# ENGLISH BISHOPS
# AT THE COUNCIL

## THE THIRD SESSION OF VATICAN II

# ENGLISH BISHOPS AT THE COUNCIL

## THE THIRD SESSION OF VATICAN II

Edited by

### MONSIGNOR DEREK WORLOCK

With a Preface by
### CARDINAL JOHN HEENAN
*Archbishop of Westminster*

LONDON
BURNS & OATES

*This arrangement copyright © Burns & Oates Ltd., 1965*

Catalogue No.: 5/4286

MADE AND PRINTED IN GREAT BRITAIN BY
BILLING AND SONS LTD, GUILDFORD AND LONDON
FOR BURNS AND OATES LIMITED,
25 ASHLEY PLACE, LONDON, S.W.1

# PREFACE

by

CARDINAL JOHN HEENAN

*Archbishop of Westminster*

THIS book is highly original. It does not pretend to tell inside stories. Intelligent readers take for granted that if anyone were really to give the inside story he would have to betray confidences. Some who published accounts of the earlier sessions of the Vatican Council were pitifully anxious to make dramatic disclosures about the intrigues, the alleged background to the debates in St. Peter's.

When journalists write books they cannot help arranging facts around theory. It is the method of their trade. Those who have written about the Council have usually employed the same model for their picture. Here are the vital statistics of the model—1500 mitred peasants (reactionaries), 600 brilliant prelates (progressives), 200 curialists.

Popular accounts of the Council have not been written in novel form but all have been to some extent works of fiction. Nobody realizes this more keenly than bishops who were members of conciliar commissions. Of these bishops none, so far as I know, has disclosed information received at commission meetings. The oath of secrecy does not rest lightly on bishops. But, notoriously, there were serious leakages of secret information to the Press.

The difficulty of counteracting the harmful effects of irresponsible disclosure is that almost always it would involve a fresh breach of confidence. Let me quote an actual example: Somebody revealed to the American Press what the Secretariat for Christian Unity intended to propose to the third session of the Vatican Council regarding the Jews. A document proposed to the Council is not altogether unlike a Bill presented to Parliament. It has certain clauses which its promoters are prepared to drop and other passages which they confidently expect will, after debate, be expanded and strengthened. So it is with the commissions which prepare schemata for debate in St. Peter's. Their task as promoters of a schema becomes impossible unless their deliberations are confidential.

It is not always possible to counteract the false impressions. In some accounts of previous sessions of the Council, Roman gossip, articles by theologians and actual speeches made in the Council were indiscriminately used to weave the pattern of the story. Some writers told you exactly what the Pope said to the Cardinal Secretary of State or Cardinal Bea. How can reports of conversations be corrected without breach of confidence by the cardinals or their friends? The parable of the cockle and the wheat has relevance to some versions of the history of former sessions of the Council. It is impossible to uproot the cockle when it is so close to the wheat. I have no doubt that a great deal more cockle has been sown and will be produced when, in coming weeks, the story of the third session is told.

That is the reason for this book. Mgr. Worlock does not set out to reveal secrets. He gives no inside stories. He is content to let the genuine and unexpurgated drama of the third session take the stage. You will not find here accounts of the dealings of the English hierarchy with the Holy Father. You will not be given any account of the many private meetings in which bishops of many nations took part.

You will read in this book an account of the Council which can be verified in every detail. After you have finished reading you will be in a position to take in your stride the flood of books on the third session which are bound to appear before the start of the final session. Monsignor Worlock has produced this book so that priests and people may have a balanced view of recent events in Rome and a true picture of the English contribution to the work of the third session. All intelligent Catholics in this country should read this straightforward, stimulating and often exciting book.

# EDITOR'S NOTE

ANYONE actively engaged in the work of the Second Vatican Council has long ago discovered the many difficulties involved in trying to explain it all to others outside Rome. The atmosphere of the debate and the more original of the speeches of the Fathers make better copy for the popular Press than the official documentation emerging from the Council. Yet in the long run it is the latter which will bring full effect to the *aggiornamento* in the Church.

The three sessions of the Council have been so packed with incident and so numerous have been the speeches that inevitably many important utterances have never seen print. This is not a difficulty peculiar to the English Bishops, though it is one which this book sets out to remedy, at least in part. But this is not intended to be a profound and comprehensive study of the Third Session. If it is coloured, it is because of the intended emphasis on the role played by the Fathers from England and Wales.

The first part of this book has its origin in a series of reports broadcast from Vatican Radio. This account of the session has deliberately been left in the form of weekly summaries in the hope that this may better reflect the impressions formed as the Session progressed.

Next the book contains the full texts of the speeches delivered in St. Peter's by the English Fathers and by the English lay auditor, Patrick Keegan. I have thought it well to include also some of the basic texts used by speakers at the weekly Press Conferences arranged by the Information Office of the Hierarchy of England and Wales. Last and by no means least, there are included for their obvious importance the opening and closing addresses of the session delivered by His Holiness Pope Paul VI.

DEREK WORLOCK

# CONTENTS

# I. OPENING OF THE THIRD SESSION

*Address of His Holiness Pope Paul VI,*
*14th September 1964*

UNDER THE sign of the Holy Cross, in whose honour we have concelebrated Holy Mass, we open today the Third Session of the Second Ecumenical Vatican Council.

The Church is present here. We are the Church. We are the Church as members of the Mystical Body of Christ, for God has granted us the inestimable favour of being baptized, of being believers united by love and constituting the consecrated and visible People of God. We are the Church since we are ministers of the Church herself, priests invested with a special character received at our sacramental ordination. On us are conferred marvellous and tremendous powers, making of us a hierarchy entrusted with functions meant to perpetuate in time and to extend on earth the saving mission of Christ. We are the Church, finally, because as teachers of the faith, pastors of souls, stewards of the mysteries of God (1 Cor. 4.1), we represent here the entire Church, not as delegates or deputies of the faithful towards whom our ministry is directed, but as Fathers and Brothers who personify the communities entrusted to the care of each one of us, and as a plenary assembly legitimately convoked by the Holy Father. The Pope has called the Council into session in his capacity, which links him with all of you, as your brother, the bishop of historic Rome, and as the humble but authentic Successor of the Apostle Peter—before whose tomb we are devoutly gathered—and therefore as the unworthy but true Head of the Catholic Church and Vicar of Christ, servant of the servants of God.

13

Recapitulating in our persons and in our functions the universal Church, we proclaim this Council ecumenical: here is the exercise of unity, here the exercise of that universality by which the Church gives evidence of her prodigious vitality, her marvellous capacity to make men brothers and to welcome within her embrace the most diverse civilizations and languages, the most individualized liturgies and types of spirituality, the most varied expressions of national, social and cultural genius, harmonizing all in felicitous union, yet always respecting legitimate variety and complexity.

Here is the exercise of the holiness of the Church because here she calls on the mercy of God, for the weaknesses and deficiencies of the sinners that we are, and because here as nowhere else do we become aware of the power granted to our ministry to draw from the "unfathomable riches of Christ" (Eph. 3.8) the treasures of salvation and sanctification for all men; here we realize that this ministry of ours has no other purpose than to "prepare for the Lord a perfect people" (Lk. 1.17). There, finally, is made manifest the apostolicity of the Church, a prerogative which is a marvel even to us, to us who have experienced our own weakness and who know how history bears witness to the frailty of even the most powerful of human institutions; and at the same time we know with what continuity and fidelity the mandate of Christ has been transmitted from the Apostles to our lowly and ever-astonished persons; we know how inexplicably and how triumphantly the Church has endured throughout the ages, this Church which is ever living and always capable of finding in herself the irrepressible spirit of youth.

At this point we can repeat with Tertullian: "It is the whole Christian world which is here represented and which we venerate. And see how good it is that from all sides men are gathered because of faith in

Christ! See how good and happy it is for brothers to dwell together!" (*De ieiuniis*, c. XIII.

Now if the Church is here, here also is the Spirit, the Advocate, whom Christ promised to His Apostles for the building up of the Church: "I will ask the Father and he will give you another Advocate to dwell with you forever, the Spirit of truth whom the world cannot receive, because it neither sees him nor knows him. But you shall know him, because he will dwell with you, and be in you . . ." (Jn. 14.16-17). For there are, as we know, two factors which Christ has promised and arranged in different ways to continue His Mission, to extend in time and on earth the Kingdom He founded and to make of redeemed mankind His Church, His Mystical Body, His fullness, in expectation of His definitive and triumphant return at the end of time: these two factors are the apostolate and the Spirit. The apostolate is the external and objective factor; it forms the material body, so to speak, of the Church and is the source of her visible and social structures. The Holy Spirit is the internal factor who acts within each person, as well as on the whole community, animating, vivifying, sanctifying.

These two agents, the apostolate which is entrusted to the sacred Hierarchy, and the Spirit of Jesus, which uses the Hierarchy as its ordinary instrument in the ministry of the Word and the Sacraments, co-operate with one another. Pentecost shows them wonderfully linked at the beginning of the great work of Jesus, who although invisible remains ever present in His apostles and their successors, "whom He set over His Church as His shepherds and vicars" (Preface of Apostles). These two agents, differently yet harmoniously, bear equal witness to Christ the Lord in a combination that confers on apostolic activity its supernatural force (cf. 1 Peter 1.12).

May we believe that this salvific plan, by which the Redemption of Christ reaches and is fulfilled in us, is even now in action? Yes, my Brethren, we must believe, indeed, that this plan is continued and actuated by our means, in virtue of a power and sufficiency that comes from God, "who has made us fit ministers of the new convenant, not of the letter but of the spirit . . . which gives life" (2 Cor. 3.6). To doubt this would be an insult to Christ's faithfulness to His promises, a betrayal of our apostolic mandate, a depriving the Church of her certainty, which the divine Word has guaranteed and history has confirmed, and of her indefectibility.

The Spirit is here. Not yet to confirm with sacramental grace the work which all of us, united in the Council, are bringing to completion, but rather to illuminate and guide our labours to the benefit of the Church and all mankind. The Spirit is here. We call upon Him, wait for Him, follow Him. The Spirit is here.

Let us reflect on this doctrine and this present reality so that, above all, we may realize once more and in the fullest and sublimest degree possible our communion with the living Christ: it is the Spirit who joins us to Him. Let us reflect on this truth also so that we may put ourselves before Him in trepidation, fully at His disposal; that we may become aware of the humiliating emptiness of our misery and the crying need we have of His help and mercy; that we may hear as if spoken in the secret recesses of our soul the words of the Apostle: "Discharging this ministry in accordance with the mercy shown us, we do not lose heart" (2 Cor. 4.1). The Council is for us a moment of deep interior docility, a moment of complete and filial adherence to the word of the Lord, a moment of fervent, earnest invocation and of love, a moment of spiritual exaltation. To this unique occasion the poetic words of St Ambrose apply with a special aptness: "Let us drink in joy the sober inebriation of the spirit" (Hymn at Lauds). Such for us should be this blessed time of Council.

And finally We have this to say: the hour has sounded in history when the Church, which expresses herself in us and from us receives structure and life, must say of herself what Christ intended and willed her to be, and what the age-long meditation of the Fathers, Pontiffs and Doctors in their wisdom has explored with piety and fidelity. The Church must give a definition of herself and bring out from her true consciousness the doctrine which the Holy Spirit teaches her, according to the Lord's promise: "But the Paraclete, the Holy Spirit, whom the Father will send in my name, he will teach you all things and bring to your mind whatever I have said to you" (Jn. 14.26). "The Spirit himself bears witness to our spirit that we are the sons of God" (Rom. 8.16). Thus must be completed the doctrine that the First Vatican Council was preparing to enunciate, but which external obstacles prevented it from defining, except in its first part dealing with the head of the Church, the Roman Pontiff, and his sovereign prerogatives regarding primacy of jurisdiction and infallibility of teaching, which Christ was pleased to bestow upon the Apostle Peter, his visible Vicar on earth, and upon those who succeed him in so sublime and tremendous an office.

The discussion on this doctrine remains to be completed, so as to explain the mind of Christ on the whole of His Church and especially on the nature and function of the successors of the Apostles, that is of the Episcopate, with which dignity and office the greater part of you, Venerable Fathers, and We Ourselves, Most Reverend Brothers, are by God's good pleasure invested.

B

The Council has many other important subjects to treat of, but this one seems to Us to be the weightiest and most delicate. The Council's deliberations on this subject will certainly be what distinguishes this solemn and historic synod in the memory of future ages. It must undertake a number of difficult theological discussions; it must determine the nature and mission of the Pastors of the Church; it must discuss, and with the favour of the Holy Spirit decide, the constitutional prerogatives of the Episcopate; it must delineate the relations between the Episcopate and the Holy See; it must show how homogeneous is the constitutional idea of the Church under its differing Eastern and Western expressions; it must make clear for the faithful of the Catholic Church and also for the separated brethren the true notion of the hierarchical organs which "the Holy Spirit has appointed as bishops to rule the Church of God" (Acts 20.28), with unquestionably valid authority in the humble and patient service of the brethren, as becomes Pastors, ministers, that is, of faith and charity.

These thoughts are all the more important for Us, and certainly for you, Venerable Brothers, because of the fact that this third session of the Ecumenical Council has chosen from among its many concerns this central objective: to investigate and clarify the doctrine of the nature of the Church, thus resuming and integrating the work done in the first two sessions, and making this solemn Synod the logical continuation of the First Vatican Council. At this point the Church wants to study itself, or rather probe into the mind of Christ, its divine Founder: just what and how much to say in order to honour His wisdom and charity and, by restoring to Him the full practice of its faith and fidelity, to render itself an even more fit instrument in the work of salvation for which it was founded.

But let no one think that in doing this the Church is

closing in on itself in an attitude of complacency, forgetting on the one hand Christ, from whom it receives everything and to whom it owes everything, or on the other hand humanity, to whose service it is committed. It places itself between Him and the world, not satisfied with itself, not as a forbidding barrier, not as an end in itself, but deeply concerned to be completely the Church of Christ, in Christ, for Christ, as well as completely the Church of men, among men, for men: humble and yet glorious, the Church of the Saviour and yet reaching out to all men, preserving and yet diffusing the truth and the grace of the supernatural life.

In our time which seems to be blessed in a special way, this seems to be all the more true and important, for today the enquiry concerning the Church will have a point of great interest for Us, and especially for you, namely the hierarchic structure of the Church itself, and consequently the origin, nature, function and power of the Episcopate, which is a major part of the hierarchy, in which with Us "the Holy Spirit has made you bishops . . . to keep watch . . . over God's Church" (Acts 20.28).

And so We have it in mind to be in tune with a plan of divine Providence in celebrating this historic moment by giving to you, Our venerated and beloved brothers in the Episcopate, the honour which our Lord desired to be shown to the Apostles together with Peter.

The Fathers of the First Vatican Council defined and proclaimed the truly unique and supreme powers conferred by Christ on Peter and handed on to his successors. This recognition has appeared to some as having limited the authority of bishops, the successors of the Apostles and as having rendered superfluous and prevented the convocation of a subsequent Ecumenical Council, which, however, according to Canon Law, has supreme authority over the entire Church. The

present Ecumenical Synod is certainly going to confirm
the doctrine of the previous one regarding the prerogatives of the Roman Pontiff. But it will also have as
its principal objective the task of describing and honour-
ing the prerogatives of the Episcopate. Let everyone
understand that the convocation of this Council has
been a free and spontaneous act on the part of Our
Venerated Predecessor, of happy memory, John XXIII,
an act which We have readily confirmed knowing full
well that the theme of this sovereign and sacred assembly would deal with the Episcopate. It could not have
been otherwise taking into consideration not only the
proper interconnection of the doctrines concerned but
also because of a sincere determination to proclaim the
glory, the mission, the merits and the friendship of Our
brothers entrusted with the work of instructing, sanctifying and governing the Church of God.

Let Us repeat as Our own those well-known words
which Our distant and saintly predecessor of immortal
memory, Gregory the Great, wrote to Eulogius,
Bishop of Alexandria: "My honour is the honour of the
universal Church. My honour is the strength of my
brothers. I am thus truly honoured when the honour
due to each and everyone of them is not denied to them."

The integrity of Catholic truth now calls for a clarification consonant with the doctrine of Papacy which
will place in its splendid light the role and mandate of
the Episcopate. In its work of tracing the outlines of
such a role and such a mandate, the Council will be
anxious about nothing except interpreting the thought
of Jesus Christ at its true source and genuine origin. We
have already had the pleasure of recognizing in the
bishops Our true brothers, addressing them, as the
Apostle Peter did, as "elders", and gladly claiming for
Ourselves the equivalent title of "fellow elder" (1 Peter
5.1). We have had the pleasure of addressing to them

the words of the Apostle Paul: "my partners in tribulations and consolations" (cf. 2 Cor. 1.7). We have been anxious to reassure them of those religious convictions that characterize Our relations with them: esteem, affection, solidarity. We are bound by Our duty to recognize them as the teachers, rulers, and sanctifiers of the Christian people, the "stewards of the mysteries of God" (cf. 1 Cor. 4.1), the witnesses to the Gospel, the ministers of the New Testament, and, in a certain sense, the very reflection of the glory of the Lord (cf. 2 Cor. 3.6–18).

As successors of Peter and, therefore, as possessors of full power over the entire Church, We have the duty of heading the body of the Episcopate, although We are surely unworthy of this dignity. Nevertheless, Our position in no way defrauds you, Our brother bishops, of your due authority. On the contrary, We are among the first to respect that sacred authority. If Our apostolic duty obliges Us to impose restrictions, to define terminology, to prescribe modes of action, to regulate the methods which concern the exercise of episcopal authority, you realize that this is done for the good of the entire Church, for the unity of that Church which has proportionately greater need of centralized leadership as its world-wide extension becomes more complete, as more serious dangers and more pressing needs threaten the Christian people in the varying circumstances of history, and, We may add, as more rapid means of communication become operative in modern times. No one should regard as a device formulated by pride such centralization, which will surely be always tempered and balanced by an alert and timely delegation both of authority and of facilities for local pastors. We assure you, Our brothers in the Episcopate, that this centralization is rather a service and a manifestation of the unifying and hierarchical spirit of the

Church. It is the glory, the power, the beauty which Christ promised to His Church and which He gradually grants to it as the ages run their course.

Apropos of this topic, We can recall the words which Pius XII, of happy memory, addressed to a certain group of bishops: "This union and this timely communication with the Holy See arises, not from a kind of longing to achieve centralization and homogeneity, but rather from the divine law itself and from a truly fundamental principle affecting the very essence of the Church of Christ" (*A.A.S.*, 1954, p. 676).

Such centralization strengthens rather than weakens the authority of bishops, whether that authority be considered in the individual bishop or in the collegiality of the bishops. How deeply We admire, how staunchly We support the rights and duties proper to the sacred hierarchy, which is the very instrument, born of the charity of Christ, and fashioned by Him to complete, to communicate, and to safeguard the integral and fruitful transmission of the treasures of faith, of example, of precepts, and of favours bequeathed by Christ to His Church. The hierarchy is the mother of the community of the faithful; it is the architect of its visible framework; it is the public representative which wins for the Church the titles of Mother and Teacher; it is the bearer of the riches of the sacraments, the conductor of the symphony of prayer, the inspiration of works of charity. Placed at the head of this sacred institution, how could We fail to devote to it Our solicitude, Our trust, Our support? How could We fail to defend it? What duty presses upon Us with greater frequency, with graver consequence, or with deeper satisfaction than that of safeguarding the independence, the freedom, the dignity of the sacred hierarchy throughout the world? Is it not true that this exhausting task has been the very fabric of which has been woven the tapestry of the history of the papacy, especially in these years of political upheavals?

Let Us add one further thought to this tribute to the Episcopate in order to show how much its intrinsic nobility and its effective charity are enhanced by the harmonious unity which must bind it in close union with the Apostolic See, and how much the Apostolic See needs you, Venerable Brothers.

For your part, dispersed as you are all over the world, if you are to give shape and substance to the true catholicity of the Church, you have the need of a centre, a principle of unity in faith and communion, a unifying power, such as, in fact, you find in this chair of Peter. Similarly, We need to have you always nearby, to give more fully to the countenance of the Apostolic See its beauty, its human and historic reality, even to give harmony to its faith, to be an example in the fulfilment of its duties, and a consolation in its times of stress.

Thus, whilst We look forward to the clearer definition which the Council's deliberations will give to the doctrine of the Episcopacy, We here and now pay you honour, pledge to you Our affection as Brother and Father, and ask of you co-operation and support. May the communion, which binds together the Catholic Hierarchy in living faith and charity, emerge from this Council deeper, stronger and more holy. It will be to the glory of Christ, the peace of the Church and the light of the world.

There is much more We would like to say on this question and on many others of the first importance which have been brought up for the attention of the Council, but We do not wish to tax your patience.

However, We cannot forgo the pleasure of sending a special greeting at this moment from this Holy See to the various dioceses and parishes whom you represent here. And first of all to our beloved and esteemed priests who labour so unselfishly in collaboration with their bishops. And to religious, striving for every perfection that will make them like Christ and serviceable to their fellow men. To the Catholic laity, working with the hierarchy for the good of the Church and for the good of society. To the poor, the persecuted and the suffering. And especially to those whom the lack of freedom still prevents from coming to this Council.

We wish, also, to welcome the auditors here present: their high ideals and outstanding merits are no secret to Us. And We are delighted to welcome among the auditors our beloved daughters in Christ, the first women in history to participate in a conciliar assembly. The auditors—both men and women—will not be slow to realize that behind this welcome of Ours lies Our fatherly love for all groups who make up the People of God, Our desire to give to the Christian community an ever-increasing sense of harmony, collaboration and charity.

And now We turn to you, the Observers, with reverence and esteem, for you have once more accepted Our invitation to attend the Council. We welcome and thank you. We wish to assure you once more of Our purpose and hope to be able one day to remove every obstacle, every misunderstanding, every hesitancy that still prevents us from feeling fully "of one heart and one soul" in Christ, in His Church (Acts 4.32). For Our part, We shall do all that possibilities allow to this end. We are fully aware that the restoration of this unity is something of no small moment, and We shall give it all the attention and the time that it calls for. It is something new, in contrast with the long, sad history which led up to the various separations, and We shall wait patiently for the conditions to ripen that will make possible a positive and friendly solution. It is something, too, of deepest significance, having its roots in the mysterious counsels of God, and We shall strive, in humility and faith, to dispose Ourselves to deserve so great a grace. We recall the words of the Apostle Paul, who brought the gift of the Gospel to all nations, seeking to become "all things to all men" (1 Cor. 9.22)—such an adaptability as we might today be tempted to call "pluralism in practice"; at the same time We recall how the same apostle has exhorted us to "preserve the unity of the Spirit in the bond of peace" because there is only "one Lord, one faith, one baptism, one God and Father of all" (cf. Eph. 4.3, 5–6).

We shall therefore strive, in loyalty to the unity of Christ's Church, to understand better and to welcome all that is genuine and admissible in the different Christian denominations that are distinct from Us; and at the same time We beg of them to try to understand the Catholic faith and life better and, when We invite them to enter into the fullness of truth and charity which, as an unmerited blessing but a formidable responsibility, Christ has charged Us to preserve, We beg them not to take it in bad part, but as being prompted by respect and brotherly love. For that fullness of truth and charity will be made the more manifest when all those who profess the name of Christ are reassembled into one.

Meanwhile, through you, Our reverend and esteemed guests and Observers in this Council, We wish to send Our cordial greetings to the various Christian communities which you represent. May Our respectful regard reach those too which are not represented here. We gather together in Our prayer and Our affections all those members who are still parted from the full spiritual and visible wholeness of the mystical Body of Christ; and in this yearning of Our love and concern, Our sorrow grows, Our hopes increase. Churches that are so far and yet so close to Us. Churches for whom

Our heart is filled with longing. Churches, the nostalgia of Our sleepless nights. Churches of Our tears and of Our desire to do you honour by Our embrace in the sincere love of Christ. May you hear, sounding from this keystone of unity, the tomb of Peter apostle and martyr, and from this Ecumenical Council of brotherhood and peace, the loving cry We send you. Maybe great distances separate us yet. Maybe it will be long before our full and effective meeting can be realized. But know for sure that already We hold you in Our heart. May the God of mercies support this Our deeply felt yearning and hope.

And finally may Our thoughts go out to the world about us, with its own interests, with its indifference too, perhaps even its hostility. We renew the greeting which We addressed to it from Bethlehem with Our resolute purpose of placing the Church at the service of its spiritual salvation and of its social prosperity, to bring it peace and true happiness.

We invite you all now, Venerable Brothers, to call upon the Holy Spirit together, as We make ready to inaugurate the third session of this Second Council of the Vatican, and in the name of the Lord, with trust in the help of Mary most holy and of the holy apostles Peter and Paul, We bestow upon you all Our apostolic blessing.

# II. THIRD SESSION SURVEY

*Broadcast Talks by Right Reverend
Monsignor Derek Worlock*

# 1. THE WEEK BEFORE

*10th September 1964*

"OTHER QUESTIONS", said Pope Paul, after out lining the achievements of the second session of the Council, "are still subject to further study and discussion. We hope that the third session in the autumn of next year will bring them to completion."

It was the closing ceremony on 4th December 1963. The Fathers had come to the end of a session which the Holy Father had described as laborious but enjoying freedom of expression. Even though only two Constitutions had emerged—the Liturgy and Mass-Media— much progress had been made on various other topics. True, certain journalists were already marking down the second session as a failure, at least humanly speaking. But they were taking scant account of the value of the long-drawn-out debates which were a necessary preliminary for the achievement of an agreed policy. Nor had they regard for the educational value of these discussions and of the opinions expressed: educational not merely for the Fathers by whom, under the repeatedly sought guidance of the Holy Spirit, the votes would have to be cast; but educational for all the people of God, spread throughout the world, upon whom the distant ripples of the Council in Rome were beginning to break.

Only two Constitutions to date. But who could say that the Church, after Pope John's call for an *aggiornamento*, would ever be the same?

The reactions to Pope Paul's forecast that perhaps the general sessions of the Council could be completed by 1964 were many and various. One immediate feeling, widely shared at the end of the hard-worked ten-week stint, was one of relief. Long absences of the bishops from their dioceses, as the Pope pointed out, could not be protracted indefinitely. For the pastors could not long be removed from their flocks. But once the excitement had died down and a little hard arithmetic had taken place, there were many others who felt that it would be a pity to spoil the rejuvenated barque of Peter for a ha'p'orth of Conciliar tar. And how could the full fruits of what had begun so brilliantly be achieved in only one more ten-week session?

It had taken two such sessions to cope with only half-a-dozen subjects. How could the remaining ten schemata (since shown to have been thirteen) be dealt with in a mere ten weeks?

It should be noted here that some months later the Holy Father referred to the possibility that there might well have to be a fourth session, perhaps in 1965. But there can be no doubt that this earlier indication of his wishes had the effect of encouraging the various Commissions to re-study their material yet again and treat the whole of their task with the utmost urgency.

In that same speech of 4th December 1963, the Pope had indicated a possible new method. The Commissions should try to prepare "in accordance with the words of the Fathers, as expressed in the general congregations, propositions profoundly studied, accurately formulated, and suitably condensed and abbreviated, so that the discussion, while remaining always free, may be rendered easier and more brief".

In other words, wherever possible, the stage where there was customarily long-drawn-out debate on a particular schema should be eliminated and the Commissions should endeavour to draw up a series of propositions upon which, after brief explanation, a vote could swiftly be taken.

How in fact has it worked out? There seems to be no doubt that some of the Commissions have felt unable to adopt this method. For several years their members and consultors have sought to present their distilled wisdom and experience in schemata which even after the first session they had already reduced in length. To attempt, even before the subject had been discussed in St Peter's, to produce succinct propositions would in their opinion reduce valuable documentation to the level of a lowest common denominator, acceptable to all but almost valueless for reasons of over-simplification. It seems likely, therefore, that from some of the Commissions schemata for general debate may still be expected.

On the other hand, where the subject-matter has already been discussed by the Fathers it has been a relatively simple task to prepare draft propositions, in the form of a Constitution. Further, there have been certain other matters—particularly legalistic matters of discipline—which it has proved possible to present as a series of propositions: more abbreviated, it is true, than if they were presented in schematic form but adequate for the presentation of Conciliar recommendations on the subject in question.

It will be seen, therefore, that when the Council Fathers reassemble in Rome for the third session of Vatican II, they will be confronted with a mixed Agenda: schemata to be debated prior to the preparation of draft decrees, which must further be voted upon and revised before a Constitution may ultimately be presented; propositions which, after brief explanation, will be submitted for vote; and Constitutions epitomizing previous debates upon matters which have already been before the Fathers in St Peter's. Doubtless some general statement on the Agenda and methods of procedure may be expected. But there is bound to be some departure from the methods employed in the previous sessions.

It has been reported that, whereas in the past a Father wishing to speak in a general congregation has had to submit his text three days in advance, he must now turn in his proposed address five days in advance. Experience suggests that this can lead only to a series of unrelated speeches, not calculated to enhance profitable debate and exchanges of opinion. Other methods are bound to be put forward. And it seems likely that where straightforward propositions are concerned, the Moderators or the Commission of Presidents may well appoint qualified spokesmen to set before the Fathers the various viewpoints about the matters concerned. It seems probable also that national hierarchies or regional groups of bishops will be asked to appoint individual speakers to advance their view in a representative capacity.

Can we also expect to see the employment of a guillotine controlling the length of discussion of any specific point? Guillotine or closure motion, the experience of the last two sessions suggests that such methods will be more apparent in the last weeks of the session than at the beginning. As is the case with all conferences, time itself is a not inconsiderable factor. Discussions tend after a while to develop a certain holy speed.

What are likely to be the main debating-points this time? The Holy Father made it clear last December that an early subject to be debated further this autumn would be the outstanding question of Revelation, a subject which occupied so much time in the first session in 1962. The document on the Church is also to be reviewed and the whole question of collegiality and the pastoral rule of dioceses. We may expect to hear more in this connection of national and regional episcopal conferences and the measure of their juridical authority.

It seems that at least thirteen documents will be included in the agenda, ranging from such subjects as Ecumenism and the Eastern Churches to the Lay Apostolate, the sacrament of marriage and the training of candidates for the priesthood. These alone could easily occupy the Fathers till the end of November. And there remains the now famous Schema XVII, advanced in order to Schema XIII, on the role of the Church in the World Today. It has rightly been said that this schema, if it is to be in any way comprehensive, might be the subject of a whole Council in itself. In fact it is likely to take the form of a Conciliar Constitution in fairly general terms, backed up by a number of Annexes dealing with matters in greater detail— though the Conciliar authority of these additional papers is not yet clear.

More than enough to get on with, you may say. Certainly the importance of this next session cannot be over-stressed. Can it be the final session for which the bishops of the Universal Church are now re-assembling in Rome? Much must depend on the new methods of procedure. But one suspects that the optimists who are saying, "It will all be over by Christmas", are likely to be wrong again. It could only be achieved if the vast majority of the work were handed over to post-conciliar Commissions. And from what has gone before it seems unlikely that the Fathers have progressed far enough to be eager yet to hand over so much important and uncompleted work.

C

## 2. THE FIRST WEEK

### *19th September 1964*

GOING BACK to the Council in Rome nowadays is just like going back to school. Routine has been established. There has been plenty of home-work. And there will be no shortage of documents to be read and lectures to be attended. By now you know the faces of many of the other pupils and there are always a certain number of new boys—consecrated since the last session—to give added interest. A series of "hard day's nights" lies ahead. This time, on arriving at the outskirts of Rome after a journey of a thousand miles, I even caught myself looking at my watch and wondering if there was still time for a last cigarette before clocking in at the Venerable English College, which is to be my base for the next ten weeks.

A third term is usually a summer term and this third session of the Council has opened in blazing heat. Mind you, we have started a fortnight earlier than last year in the hope of finishing this stint in time to enable those who wish to go on to the Eucharistic Congress in Bombay. It has also meant that the students at the colleges where most of the Fathers stay are still out of Rome on vacation. The organization men have had to make adaptations.

There has already been much talk as to whether this third session can be the last, whether the Fathers can complete the massive agenda which resulted from Pope John's throwing the questions to be discussed wide open. Although just now it is not difficult to be patient about long and repetitive speeches as yet undelivered, one senses a determination to achieve positive results before the end of term. But whilst there is every desire to avoid the pitfalls of a sluggish procedure, most of the Fathers seem to have accepted that, if the consideration of material is to be other than perfunctory, this session properly conducted is likely to be the penultimate rather than the last. And even then the pressure will have to be on.

As we sweltered in St Peter's for the solemn opening of the session on Monday last, 14th September, no one thought of using the phrase "turning on the heat". It is perhaps hard to believe that a Basilica of that size can become as muggy and stifling as the atmosphere in an overcrowded mission-hut. We assembled at 8.30 a.m. and by the time Pope Paul made his entry soon after 9 a.m., handkerchiefs were out, not to wave greetings, but to mop up perspiring brows.

The Pope himself, vested in a wine-red velvet chasuble, looked a lot cooler than the twenty-four bishops with whom he was to concelebrate the Mass and who were almost enveloped in chasubles, gothic and full. These Fathers of the Council included three Cardinals whose selection was of interest in that the ceremonial carried out was in itself an innovation—though some would claim that it was a return to the past. The Dean of the Sacred College, Cardinal Tisserant, the President of the Liturgical Concilium, Cardinal Lercaro, and the Prefect of the Sacred Congregation of Rites, Cardinal Larraona: these make a formidable trio at the best of times. But with the Pope concelebrating with them, who could say that the idea of concelebration lacked the full backing of ecclesiastical top brass? As for the others, it goes without saying that they were of every colour and continent—with the Benedictine Abbot Primate and the Superior General of the Carmelites thrown in for good measure.

His Holiness came to the foot of the Papal altar to commence the soon-to-disappear Psalm 42. Two and a half thousand bishops thundered back the response: dialogue at its most impressive. The Introit was sung by all to a simple tone, the *Kyrie* and *Gloria* were in plainsong, the Pope monotoned a prayer, the Carmelite chanted the Epistle, Cardinal Tisserant sang the Gospel and the choir led the singing of the Creed. At this stage the uninitiated were still unsure if it was High Mass, Low Mass or *Missa Cantata*. But perhaps one should say just that it was Solemn Mass with singing. At all events participation was active and impressive.

The concelebrants all received a portion of the Sacred Host, the geometric proportions of which defied me. They all communicated from the same large chalice and the lay auditors came forward to receive Communion from the Holy Father himself. It was approaching 10.30 when, with the Pope's blessing, the Mass ended. Perhaps, always allowing for local accommodations, this was the shape of things to come. But the emphasis given by this wonderful concelebration of Mass to the whole notion of Collegiality, the sharing by the bishops in the authority of the Church, set the theme for the session and for the Pope's allocution which followed.

The hour had come, said Pope Paul, when the Church must give a definition of herself and bring out from her true consciousness the doctrine which the Holy Spirit taught her. "Thus must be completed the doctrine that the First Vatican Council was preparing to enunciate, but which external obstacles prevented it from defining, except in its first part dealing with the head of the Church, the Roman Pontiff, and his sovereign prerogatives . . . The discussion of this doctrine remains to be completed, to explain the mind of Christ on the whole of His Church and especially on the nature and function of the successors of the apostles . . . the Episcopate, with which dignity and office the greater part of you, Venerable Fathers, and We Ourselves, Most Reverend Brothers, are by God's good pleasure invested."

In these few words the Pope summed up what was to be perhaps the most important issue of the session. It must see the definition of the role and prerogatives of the bishops, whilst at the same time leaving secure the unchallengeable primacy of the See of Peter. And having carefully and delicately re-stated that primacy, the Pope went on to extol the importance of the role of the individual bishop and of the Episcopate as a body. Centralization in the leadership of the Church was a necessary manifestation of the unifying and hierarchical spirit of the Church. But that relationship needed a closer study and delineation which must be achieved in the weeks ahead.

The Holy Father's words were themselves history and would require closer study than was possible in the now turgid heat of the Basilica. For three-quarters of an hour the Pope addressed the assembly, something he will not normally do again until the end of the session. It was important that the pattern and the mandate be established. In conclusion he sent a message of affectionate greeting to all the priests and parishes of the world. He added a word of welcome to the lay auditors and, though his words appeared premature in that the chosen twelve there present were the same as for the last session, he told the Fathers that he was "delighted to welcome among the auditors our beloved daughters in Christ, the first women in history to participate in a conciliar assembly". Perhaps it was as well that these women, whose identity has not yet been made public, were not actually present for this opening ceremony. Had they fallen victim to the heat and the stretchers been sent for once more, the more conservative heads might have nodded in a gesture other than exhaustion.

Finally, His Holiness spoke to the Observers. He moved to his peroration and in a series of parallel constructions spoke with affection of the denominations there officially represented. Somehow such oratory always seems more eloquent in Latin and the official English translation provided for the Press was literal but awkward. "Churches that are so far and yet so close to Us. Churches for whom Our heart is filled with longing. Churches, the nostalgia of Our sleepless nights. Churches of Our tears and of Our desire to do you honour by Our embrace in the sincere love of Christ . . ."

His Holiness remounted the sedia and the procession wound its way down the length of the Basilica. The Fathers made their way out into the blazing sun in St Peter's Square into their buses and into the inevitable traffic jams.

The next morning the General Congregations began. The first task was to deal with Chapter 7 of the schema "*De Ecclesia*". Introductory remarks were delivered, positions assumed and clear instructions have been given as to the methods to be employed in voting on the various issues which were under consideration. Here the General Secretariat has given clear evidence that much thought has been given as to how the points at issue can be dealt with and decisions reached without undue repetition or suppression of the freedom to speak. No doubt snags will arise, but few can have failed to value the attempt to circumvent the trials and the tribulations of the past. Few but perhaps not all.

As I left St Peter's last Tuesday, thinking of mad dogs and Englishmen out in the midday sun, a journalist stopped me and said, suitably enough with heat, "So they are going to steam-roller it through." Only a few weeks ago the same man was complaining of pointless delays. You can't please all the people all the time.

## 3. THE SECOND WEEK

### *26th September 1964*

IT IS strange how quickly one settles back into the Conciliar routine. After only a fortnight the glamour and excitement of reunion with friends soon wear off and the resumption of daily Congregations in St Peter's rapidly closes the nine months gap between sessions. Rome itself bears little outward sign of change. In spite of a vast campaign to remind citizens that noise kills, the roar of traffic continues unabated. Motor-cyclists still "rev up" their engines beneath the windows of the English College where most of the Hierarchy is housed. The College clock continues by day and by night to chime the full hour at every quarter. The cats in the *cortile* conduct their nocturnal prenuptial enquiries. But if there is any difference this time, it is that the weather is hotter than the Fathers have had to endure during either of the previous sessions.

In St Peter's itself the routine is re-established, though at about twice the normal speed. The Moderators call "Time" as soon as the speaker reaches his ten-minute limit. And that they mean business may be seen from the fact that the venerable Cardinal Bea himself came under the hammer the other day. Already one notices one consequence of this ready employment of the closure motion procedure, now set in motion just as soon as the Moderators think that the subject—and possibly the patience of the Fathers—is exhausted. There seems to be far more representative speaking. Up to a point this is a good thing. If whole Hierarchies can entrust their views to an individual spokesman, much needless repetition is avoided. But it does mean a preponderance of speakers from the Sacred College of Cardinals, who still have the right to first "go" at the microphone each morning. And if they have no Cardinal amongst their number, groups of bishops inevitably tend to put up their senior man, because the higher he is in the seniority list the greater his chance of intervening before the debate in question is closed. This could well mean that we shall now be provided with a lesser variety of speakers than before, with the corollary that we may hear fewer of the junior bishops with their "new" outlook. This would be a pity.

There have been the inevitable cracks about the sessions having made a start with the four last things. In fact the Fathers commenced with the hitherto undiscussed remnants of the schema on the Church. Cardinal Browne, as a leader member of the Doctrinal Commission—please note the new style of address for the former Commission on Faith and Morals—introduced Chapter 7 of the document on "The eschatological nature of our vocation and our union with the Church in Heaven"—a weighty title, you'll agree. He reminded the Fathers that until the end of time the Church comprises members in Heaven, in Purgatory and on earth, and that those on earth are encouraged to strive for Heaven by the example of the saints. The pastoral consequence of this, said this giant Irish Dominican, was that the thought of the blessed in Heaven should be a stimulus to our efforts to glorify God here on earth. And in the two-day debate which followed, perhaps the most original intervention came from the Belgian Cardinal Suenens, who ploughed right into this whole question of sanctity, or, more accurately, into the official process of canonizing saints.

To spur her children to sanctity, he said, the Church sets before them the example of canonized saints. But these would be much more impressive if they were seen to represent all nations and all classes and conditions of life. He then treated us to the fruits of some interesting statistical research. Since the beginning of the eighteenth century, 85 per cent of all canonized non-martyrs came from religious orders, and 90 per cent from the continent of Europe. The process of canonization, not the spiritual fecundity of certain nations, needed revision. At the moment the process was too slow, too expensive and too centralized. He thought that the process of beatification might well be entrusted to local Episcopal Conferences. Only when devotion became truly international should the Pope proceed to canonization.

Chapter 8 of the document on the Church deals with Our Blessed Lady. And it has quite a history. It will be remembered that in the last session there were those who wanted a separate schema "*De Beata Maria Virgine*", whereas the English Bishops were to the fore in suggesting that Our Lady, as a member of the Church, should be included in the schema on the Church and not put forward as quite a separate object of devotion. So in fact it has turned out, though perhaps more important was Abbot Butler's plea that the subject be treated with biblical emphasis and using Tradition established prior to the break between East and West. This question of whether or not to include in this document a treatment of those teachings which had developed only in recent times, seems now to have settled down about the role of Our Lady as Mediatrix. And many of the contributions in St Peter's dealt with this point.

Cardinal Ruffini, for example, moved right in on this with his speech. He felt that the title of Mediatrix needed fuller explanation lest non-Catholics should imagine that we neglected the role of Christ as the one Mediator. Cardinal Wyszynski wanted the whole chapter given more prominence. Montreal's Cardinal Léger wanted the title of Mediatrix out, as it was difficult to interpret and seemed to contradict the biblical affirmation that Christ is the one Mediator. Cardinal Silva Henriquez from Chile also wanted it out and Cardinal Bea, whilst accepting the underlying doctrine, thought the matter too immature and as yet lacking scriptural argument, to be included in this chapter. Cardinal Suenens at least gave the impressions that he wanted it kept in—an impression built on his allegation that the chapter was minimalist in its assertion of Mary's spiritual maternity in the Church today.

So it goes on. In, out, in, out. I suspect that now some compromise must be found: possibly to include Mediatrix amongst the many titles of honour given to Our Lady, but without giving it the predominance or emphasis which a separate development of this teaching might involve.

There was one other speech on this subject I should mention. Archbishop Gawlina, known so well to Polish exiles for whom he had special care, said in the name of the Polish hierarchy that devotion to Our Lady was a help and not an obstacle to Ecumenism. In support of his contention he referred surprisingly enough to Martin Luther. It was a fine, stirring and scholarly speech, which made it all the harder to believe the news when it was announced last Monday that Archbishop Gawlina had died during the night. He was a patient, resolute and long-suffering son of his country, renowned as it is for devotion to Our Lady. May he now rest in peace.

After the debate on *"De Ecclesia"*, consideration passed to that subject which used to be called *"De Episcopis"* but which is now called "The Pastoral Duty of Bishops". Many people see this as the document to put teeth into the theological treatment of the Church. There is some truth in this for it deals with the organization of the Church, as well as the pastoral rule of a diocese. It gives practical form to the whole question of collegiality. One obvious way is the proposed establishment of National or Regional Episcopal Conferences with juridical power. Of course many countries, like England and Ireland, have had Bishops' Meetings for longer than we can remember. But always decisions have been reached with no more binding force as a common policy than that of a gentleman's agreement: that is, with some twenty or so diocesan bishops all agreeing as individual Ordinaries to follow a common course of action. By the new proposals a formally established Conference with a permanent Secretariat would have the power to make joint decisions, by two-thirds majority vote, and with binding force on all concerned. If there is to be delegation of power from the Holy See to National or Regional groups of bishops then this proposal seems to be a natural consequence.

But we need not think that the document deals only with organization, as may be seen from the intervention by Bishop Foley of Lancaster, making his maiden speech in the Council. He pleaded that the pastoral care of souls should receive greater emphasis, in accordance with the oft-repeated pastoral goal of the Council to renew the practice of religion especially in de-christianized areas. The priests must know their people in a manner which can only be achieved through parish visiting. An improvement in the practice of the faith would be better achieved by an intimate contact between pastor and people. The Bishop thought that the Council should come down squarely in stating this, rather than using its time exclusively in the consideration of new doctrinal theories.

The underlying theme for this session to date has been the issue of collegiality, about which many votes have so far been cast. But due to rules which sometimes mean that the Fathers have two and even three subjects under consideration at the same time we have now moved on from "The Church" and "The Bishops" to "Religious Liberty". Not surprisingly the Council produced its largest attendance this session last Wednesday when the debate on Religious Liberty began. The biggest speech of the day undoubtedly came from Cardinal Cushing. His frequent assertions in the past that the Latin language meant nothing to him put everyone at once in sympathetic vein. But manfully he made his way through his text, and who shall quarrel with the Moderators if for once they forgot to give him the warning bell when he went over time? The main tenor of the Cardinal's argument was that the Church must present herself to the world as a protagonist of religious liberty. She was quite justified in seeking the liberty of the Church in civil society for her own Hierarchy and for the whole People of God. But the Church must now assert that same liberty for other Churches and their members, indeed for every human being. If at times the Cardinal's manner of address was reminiscent of an address to thousands gathered at a rally in Boston, the applause which was accorded him would not have disgraced such a crowd of supporters.

As you can see, there has been no shortage of material for discussion. A fast pace has already been etablished and the next few weeks will show whether this can be preserved. Certainly the interest of the Press has been quite phenomenal and the various Press Conferences and briefing sessions have been packed out.

Here surely of word of praise is due to those stalwart priests who sit at the reporters' tables in St Peter's each morning and take copious notes. As the great bronze doors cascade their cargo out into the midday sun, you can see these enthusiastic characters making their way quickly to the *Ufficio Stampa* where they proceed to give fairly full summaries of what has taken place, as the journalists, divided into language groups, press about these spokesmen, struggling to present an adequate picture to the world. It is a tremendous task to carry out each day, only rivalled in my opinion by those few experts who sit each morning with the Observers and provide for them a simultaneous interpretation service. These Press spokesmen, these interpreters, are just some of the hidden heroes of the Council. They are unlikely to find their way into the annals of Church history but they are an essential part of the vast Conciliar machine.

## 4. THE THIRD WEEK

### *3rd October 1964*

THE OTHER day I had a letter from a priest friend of mine in the East End of London. "For heaven's sake", he wrote "get a move on with this Council. Remember that for us it means flesh and blood." Somehow I resisted the temptation to send him back a postcard pointing out that to most of us here in Rome, the Vatican Council has meant blood, sweat and tears. But instead I became lost in thought about the problems of communication, and about how hard it is to explain to others outside Rome that the matters being debated and decided in St Peter's just now have a vital importance to all the members of the Church, whether in Rome or in the East End of London—or for that matter in Hong Kong.

How does one begin to explain? Understand for a start that there are really two streams of activity going on in the Council simultaneously. First, there are the subjects for debate, that is, documents circulated in advance to the Bishops who speak to move amendments, as it were; and then there are also the documents which have already been debated and have now been amended and returned to the Council Chamber for vote by the Bishops. Thus each day in St Peter's there are speeches on some quite new subject, interspersed with voting on documents which were perhaps debated in the last session a year ago but have since been amended.

It sounds pretty desperately complicated but in fact it works out quite well. To think in terms of British Parliamentary procedure—and it's difficult to do that— each morning's debate (which goes on from 9 till 12.30 and is in Latin) is rather like a Second Reading of a Bill: which, after the debate, goes to a Council Commission for amendment—Committee stage, if you like— and then back to St Peter's for a kind of combined Report Stage and Third Reading. Then, if passed with the necessary two-thirds majority, it goes to the Pope for approval and promulgation—rather like the Royal Assent in Britain.

Thus this last fortnight, whilst the actual debate has been on topics like Religious Liberty, Church Unity and Divine Revelation, the voting—and sometimes there are six votes in a morning—has been on a subject debated a year ago. That subject is the structure of the Church—its make-up, not the building, you understand—and you cannot have anything much more fundamental than that. There is this advantage in the time-lag between debate and vote. Not only does it provide time for the document to be amended in the light of all the speeches, it also gives the Bishops a chance to weigh up the sometimes conflicting views they have heard.

I suppose that it is always hard to realize that you are taking part in history, especially Church history, but there is no doubt that the matter being voted on during these past three weeks of the new session is really historic. The snag is that it is all cloaked in a word which few have heard of before and fewer understand. "Collegiality". It has an ugly sound. What exactly does it mean? It means that the Bishops, as successors of the Apostles, form a College, or group, which shares power over the Universal Church. And this by divine institution.

I thought Bishop Holland of Salford put it well at a Press Conference some days ago. Christ gave his authority to the Apostles as a group, the Bishop said. Present-day Bishops are now that group. But there is no group complete without the successor of St Peter, the Pope, giving it unity and strength. The First Vatican Council in the last century carefully delineated the powers of the Head with its decree on the infallibility of the Pope. But perforce that Council broke up before going on to deal with the role of Bishops. It was like showing a head without shoulders, like showing a mountain peak without the supporting range. And now this Second Vatican Council has shown the whole range or, if you like, the shoulders from which the head of the body springs. In this respect Vatican II has completed what was begun by Vatican I.

Yes, my friend in the East End of London may say, that's all very nice and tidy. But what difference is it going to make to us?

Sharing in authority must mean delegation of power. In practical terms I think that we may look forward to a Senate of Bishops in the Church, whether representative or selected, acting of course with the Pope and discussing policy with him. And it must also mean the delegation of authority to National Conferences of Bishops to deal with the local problems of their people. This would mean, amongst other things, that the Roman Curia—the central government of the Church—would become an administrative rather than a policy-making body. And that is a radical change.

Now all this has been passed by the Bishops in Council in a long series of votes on a document divided, curiously enough, into thirty-nine articles.

Incidentally, this document also made provision for mature married men to be made deacons—to help in the administration of some of the sacraments. This should be a great help in some of the mission territories. But the proposal that young men who are deacons might be allowed to marry and remain deacons was defeated last Tuesday by a very large majority. So there is no change in policy with regard to the celibacy of the clergy.

So important was this issue of collegiality that it overshadowed the other subjects being debated whilst this voting was in progress. But not entirely so. For at the end of last week the great debate on Religious Liberty began. Last Monday, Archbishop Heenan of Westminster, in a speech which won applause seldom accorded nowadays, stressed the necessity of religious liberty and freedom of conscience. As a practical example the Archbishop pointed to England where, although there is an Established Church, full religious liberty is granted to citizens of other faiths and, for instance, they receive equal financial help for their schools. "We are persuaded", he said, "that the external practice of religion should be subject only to those restrictions which are absolutely necessary to safeguard public order."

Dr Heenan has had a busy week. Last Saturday he spoke to a packed-out Press Conference on Religious Liberty and on the subject of the Council's document on the Jews. He always sparkles on these occasions and was in tremendous form in the subsequent question and answer session. On Tuesday he was up in St Peter's again to urge that the Council should, once and for all, acquit the Jewish people as such of what some call deicide. "It would certainly be unjust in our day", he argued, "to condemn all European Christians for the death of Jews in Germany and Poland. It is no less unjust to condemn the whole Jewish people for the death of Christ." The point was well-made and well-taken.

Continuing at the present spanking pace, the Fathers have now moved on to discuss Divine Revelation, the subject which caused all the fireworks two years ago. The new document is hailed by some as a brilliant synthesis of all that was said at that time, but others say that it has shirked the real issue as to the relative importance of Scripture and Tradition in the transmission of Christian Revelation. The debate goes on, but at all events the new document seems unlikely to delay the Bishops for longer than the five days scheduled for it.

Can the Council, now in its third session, complete its schedule of work before its adjournment in late November? That is the question on everyone's lips. I personally think it is too early to tell. There are many vital points still to come, including the eagerly awaited document on "The Church in the World Today". But this issue should become clearer shortly.

To end on a lighter note. It rained last Monday—the first rain we have seen since we arrived in sweltering heat three weeks ago. So there is now a spate of colds in St Peter's. And the women auditors have also arrived in St Peter's to view the proceedings. They include a number of nuns, amongst them the Mother General of the Sisters of Charity: the S.V.P. nuns or "White Wings", as they are called. Thank goodness, she has just adopted that much publicized new look, with a simple veil instead of the traditional vast white starched linen headdress. I was sitting just behind her, so I appreciated the point.

D

## 5. THE FOURTH WEEK

### *10th October 1964*

SOME DAYS ago Bishop de Smedt of Bruges remarked that no document was ever discussed by the Council Fathers in St Peter's without its being improved by amendments made in the light of debate. Whether the Bishop was thinking of battles fought and won in the past, or battles yet to come, one cannot be sure. It was he, you remember, who delivered the now famous anti-triumphalism speech in the first session just two years ago. There can be little doubt that this tremendous feat of oratory had a considerable effect on the vote which led Pope John to intervene and withdraw the document under discussion at the time, on the Sources of Revelation.

Two years have passed and just over a week ago the Fathers commenced the discussion on this much revised schema, now called quite simply Divine Revelation. This had been prepared by a special Commission appointed by the Pope. And anyone who had expected a repetition of all the excitements of November 1962 was doomed to disappointment.

In some ways the most significant difference between the two documents could be seen from the change in title. Instead of being called "The Sources of Revelation" it was now quite simply "Divine Revelation". This change reflected the fact that the new schema left open the whole question of whether revelation is to be drawn from Scripture *and* Tradition, or whether the Scripture contains, at least implicitly, the whole content of the Catholic faith.

As the Abbot of Downside pointed out, the authors of the new document had deliberately avoided committing the Council to either of these views, believing that the matter is still the subject of living controversy, and it is better to give time for these modern opinions to mature than to close the issue by a definitive statement one way or the other.

Needless to say the "Trad. Men" could not be expected to take this lying down, but even then the debate on the subject occupied only five days and the last two of these at least found most of the onlookers struggling to maintain interest during the long-drawn-out expression of technical niceties by Scriptural exegetes. And it is surprising how many there are of these nowadays.

Speaking towards the close of the debate on Tuesday, Abbot Butler left no one in doubt as to his personal feelings in this matter. "In the course of this almost miraculous Council," he said, "we have done much to drive out that spirit of fear and excessive anxiety by which at times our labours were hindered. Let us not be afraid of scholarly and historical truth. Let us not be afraid that our scholars may be lacking in loyalty to the Church and to traditional doctrine. They are loyal Catholics; and they are at the same time scientific scholars whose first presupposition is honesty of investigation. What we want is not the childish comfort which comes from averting our gaze from the truth but a truly critical scholarship which will enable us to enter into 'dialogue' with non-Catholic scholars."

The Abbot's introduction of this ecumenical note was timely, for during the first half of the week the debate had been interspersed with a series of votes on the revised document on Ecumenism. Each of the three chapters was presented for vote by a speech from one of the members of the Secretariat for Christian Unity. The third chapter, presented on Wednesday, dealt with the Churches and Ecclesiastical Communities separated from the Holy See. It was divided into two parts: the first dealing with the separated brethren of the Eastern Churches and the second with those of the West.

It seemed most suitable that the latter should be introduced by an Englishman, and the task fell to Archbishop Heenan who has taken a leading part in this most important work. He told the Fathers in St Peter's that, in preparing the new document, the Secretariat had been guided by the thought that, by showing what Christians have in common, some foundation would be provided for dialogue with our separated brethren. But it was also essential to give a clear picture of the doctrines which divide Christians. Some had thought that the earlier document on this subject smacked of proselytism, others that it might encourage indifferentism. The Secretariat had striven to meet both objections.

"The world is waiting for the outcome of this debate", said Doctor Heenan. "Here is our great opportunity of showing that it is as true today as it was in the early Church that Christians are recognizable as such because they love one another. I hope, Venerable Brethren," he concluded, "that you will show your good pleasure by recording a unanimous vote." When the count took place next day it revealed that of the two thousand one hundred and seventy Fathers present only twenty-four had voted *non placet*.

On Wednesday also began the debate on the Lay Apostolate. The Lay Auditors were present in strength when the Bishop of Essen opened the discussion, explaining on behalf of the Lay Apostolate Commission the principles which had guided its members in the preparation of the document. The main difficulty, he explained, had been to try to deal with such a vast subject in the small space permitted. Moreover the treatment of the theology of the layman had been taken out of the schema so that it could be dealt with as a chapter in the document on the Church. Much of what had been written about the role of the layman in the temporal order had been transferred to the schema on the Church in the World Today. As things stand, the document, mutilated as it may be, deals with the call to the apostolate, the various fields in which it is to be exercised, its different forms and the relationship between the laity and the Bishops in their combined response to the Mission of the Church.

As is customary procedure, the first speeches dealt with the document in general and whether it was to be accepted as a basis for debate on particular points and then revised by the Commission in the light of the observations made. Often this initial stage can occupy several days, but after only four speeches the Moderator, Cardinal Suenens, moved that it be accepted as a basic document and this was carried by a overwhelming majority.

Speeches on different aspects of the subject have continued since last Wednesday, and I would gather that it may well go on for another couple of days. Already a number of points have emerged, though inevitably some of the views expressed have been in conflict, such as "it's too long" or "it's too short". There has been praise for the section on formation for the apostolate, though many would like to see it further developed. There is recognition of the obvious effort of the Commission to provide a balance between the overall responsibility of the hierarchy and the real initiative which must be left to the laity. But though some, like Cardinal Ritter, have said that the language and approach is too clerical, there is at least pleasure that probably for the first time a Council is trying to deal with the active participation of the laity in the Mission of the Church.

Clearly the Commission is going to be busy with

amendments. But as Bishop de Smedt said, the document will be all the better for that.

I may be wrong but I gained the impression on Friday that for the first time there was some let-up in the obvious pressure which the Moderators have been most effectively bringing upon the Council proceedings during this session. So far the speed with which the debate has been conducted has been phenomenal, but on Friday the manner in which a number of speakers moved rather laboriously through points already made was reminiscent of some of the debates in the earlier sessions. Perhaps this was due to the fact that this document is the first we have had this session which has not come under discussion before. Perhaps also the Moderators were anxious to provide an opportunity for complete liberty of expression by the many Fathers who wanted to speak on this subject. Perhaps finally they had in mind that the laity themselves would expect a fair quota of time to be set aside for the discussion of a matter of such great concern to them.

But inevitably it has led to more conjecture as to whether there is to be a whole-hearted attempt to complete the work of the Council during the present session. The agenda ahead is still vast. There are all the propositions to be dealt with and there remains the outstanding question of the document on The Church in the World Today. Current opinion is that this vast subject alone could occupy the Fathers in Council for many weeks and I feel that the opinion is hardening that there will have to be a fourth session, even if only because it is likely to prove impossible for all the Commissions to complete their work of amendment and return their documents to the Council for vote by the end of the third week in November.

We shall see. In the meantime the irrepressible General Secretary, Archbishop Felici, continues in his unruffled and benign way. Each day he succeeds in finding some new form of endearing address either for the Fathers, or for the Observers, or for the Lady Auditors, and on occasion even for those who are admitted into the Mass but have to leave St Peter's when he declares with relish *"Exeant omnes"*. Perhaps his best performance this week was when, prior to a vote, he read out seventy-five lines of Latin text in just under four minutes. It was an almost operatic performance and it was only because his hearers were left gasping that he was not greeted with a burst of applause.

## 6. THE FIFTH WEEK

### *17th October 1964*

If an American were to say to you "The happiest Dixie is the Friday noonday", would you have the slightest idea what he was talking about? Would you perhaps conjure up pictures of the Deep South and of some dusky minstrel twanging away on his banjo? If so, you would be wrong. The person who made that remark to me the other day was a North American bishop here in Rome —and in connection with the Vatican Council. Let me explain. You know that all, or almost all, the speeches in St Peter's each day are delivered in Latin. It's not too bad. Your ear gets attuned to it after a while. But when the speaker has said his piece, it's customary for him to conclude by saying quite simply *"Dixi"*: which being interpreted means "I have spoken".

For most of the speakers I am sure that it's a great relief to have the carefully prepared speech off their chest. But I would not deny that after the last speaker of the morning—and there are usually about 16 or 17 of them—when he's finished and said his *"Dixi"*, the sense of relief is shared by most of his collegial brethren who gather up their papers, recite the Angelus and make their way home to lunch. And on no day is that relief and sense of hard-worked achievement more obvious than on Friday; for there are no more debates in the Aula of St Peter's until the following Monday morning.

That is why "The happiest *Dixi* is the Friday noonday". Indeed the last speaker on a Friday morning, finishing with his "I've said my piece" at about 12.30 to be precise, is not infrequently answered with *"Deo Gratias"*.

It doesn't require a great stretch of the imagination to appreciate the strain of listening to all those speeches in Latin each morning. And I won't disguise from you the fact that just now most of the Fathers—and the *periti* or experts—are pretty tired. We have been at it for exactly five weeks and according to the schedule we have another five weeks to run before the session closes. And the pace this time has been terrific. Already we have covered far more material than was dealt with in either of the other two sessions. It has meant a corresponding increase in the daily home-work. Just keeping abreast of the flood of official documents issued each day is quite an accomplishment. And apart altogether from the daily sessions in St Peter's, there is an abundance of meetings each evening of Commissions, Amendment Sub-Commissions, Language Groups, National Conferences of Bishops, and so on. During the last three weeks I have had twenty-five evening meetings, some of them lasting for three hours.

Half-way through. It's rather interesting if one looks back to the last two sessions to remember that each time at the midway stage there has been some crisis. Two years ago it was the famous debate on the Sources of Revelation. Last year it was the issue of collegiality and the famous test-votes.

I don't know whether the Press were on the look-out for symptoms last weekend or what. But quite suddenly the sense of crisis was back. Accusations were bandied about by journalists alleging undue influences being brought to bear on their favourite documents, Religious Liberty and the Jews. But none seemed quite to know where it had all started. Certainly there were many activities behind the scenes—the Press can never resist that word "Cabal"—and then on Tuesday it was all over. It was probably more than a storm in a tea-cup, but at least all the relevant assurances about these two important documents had been given. One wonders if we have heard the last of this business. But things quietened down, so that the Council might be squeezed from the pages of the newspapers by Mary Rand's gold medal, the General Election in Britain and the strange disappearance of Mr Krushchev from the international scene.

What's been going on in St Peter's this week? Last week I forecast that the debate on the Lay Apostolate would run another couple of days. So it turned out.

The debate on Monday was valuable. With regard to the set-up of Catholic Action, the document advocates a sort of *via media* and the general opinion seemed to be that local hierarchies should be left free to choose whatever structure of lay activity seemed best for their territory. There was also great emphasis on the role of the layman in the temporal order and on the work of the organized apostolate of Catholic societies in training laymen for their role in public life: membership of an organization being seen as a means rather than an end in itself. Most impressive to me was the speech of Bishop Power of Antigonish on the subject of the work of formation: a nice balance between what he called insertion in the ministry of Christ (learning utter dependence on Our Lord) and insertion in the reality of the world (learning to see events in the light of faith).

But perhaps the liveliest speech of the day came from Archbishop Heenan, speaking in the name of all the bishops of England and Wales. He pointed out that the place of laymen in the life of the Church had completely changed. In Italian the word *chiericho*, corresponding with our English "clerk", meant learned, while *idiota* was used to describe either a fool or a member of the laity. All that had now changed. He then went on to speak of the proposal to establish in Rome a Secretariat for the Lay Apostolate. "It is obviously necessary for this Secretariat to have the guidance of competent ecclesiastics," he said. "But this does not mean that all the business must be conducted by prelates. It would be a disaster to model it on any of the Departments already existing in the Roman Curia. Most of the members must be chosen from the laity and they should be men and women who in their own countries have taken a lead in the Lay Apostolate. Nor do we want to send to Rome", he added, "only old gentlemen who are loaded down with ecclesiastical honours. We must also choose some of our young men and women who have to earn their daily bread."

This speech seemed to be widely appreciated and by none more than the lay auditors. On the following day the debate wound up with an historic event which must be a source of great pride to English Catholics. Patrick Keegan, now President of the World Movement of Christian Workers, but still better known to us as the Wigan-born former Y.C.W. leader, was chosen to address the Council about the document which the Fathers had been debating. Speaking in English and keeping within the famous ten-minute time-limit, he really did quite outstandingly well. The document, he said, was the result of the progressive discovery by men and women of their responsibility and role within the whole apostolate of the Church. It marked a point of fulfilment in the historical development of the Lay Apostolate. The laity sincerely hoped that it marked also the beginning of a whole new stage of development. Appealing to the bishops for the help of priests as chaplains to lay movements, Keegan went on to say: "The Lay Apostolate cannot be an isolated entity in the Church. By its very nature it demands a constant and regular exchange between the hierarchy and the laity. It is for us as lay people to bring to our Pastors our experience of the needs of the world in which we live, and to seek from them guidance in our endeavour to respond to these needs." Afterwards it was good to see three Cardinals from the Commission of Presidents seize his hand to congratulate him as he made his way back to his place.

From the Lay Apostolate the Council Fathers passed on to the Priesthood, or the Priestly Ministry as the new document is called. Many speakers seemed to feel that with so much emphasis nowadays on the royal priesthood of the faithful, a more profound treatment might be given to the priesthood of Holy Orders. This point was brought out by Bishop Théas of Lourdes who remarked that, since many today looked upon the priest simply as a man, like unto other believers, it was necessary to proclaim that the priest by ordination receives the priesthood of Christ himself and carries out his ministry in the person of Christ. Many other speakers took the same theme. But it was Bishop Gordon Wheeler from Middlesbrough who, in a Press Conference on Thursday, remarked on the coincidence that this document should have been introduced by Archbishop Marty of Rheims. Quoting from the *Ingoldsby Legends*, he recited, "Never I ween was a prouder scene, read of

in books or dreamt of in dreams, than the Cardinal
Lord Archbishop of Rheims". "How singularly fitting",
commented the Bishop, "that the present Archbishop
of Rheims should be the Relator to a document which
condemns outmoded feudalism and the whole world of
the little jackdaw!"

Much of the last two days of the week was devoted to
the Eastern Churches and inevitably most of the speakers have been drawn from the various Oriental Rites.
There has been much discussion on the problems arising
from marriages between members of different rites. The
speaker who attracted most attention was that well-
known Conciliar figure Maximos IV, Patriarch of
Antioch of the Melchites, who delivered a vehement
defence of the rights and privileges of the various
Patriarchates. It is wrong, he claimed, to present the
Patriarchate as an institute proper to the East; it is
common to the Catholic Church, the first Patriarch of
which is the Bishop of Rome. Just as the Pope, as
Bishop of Rome, is equal to the other bishops, so also as
Patriarch of the West he is the colleague of the Patri-
archs of the East. The true concept of a Patriarchate
must be restored to the Church before there could be
hope of dialogue with the Orthodox.

Another week gone by. I think that the honours go to
the layman, Pat Keegan, for his splendid acquittal of
such a difficult task last Tuesday. Shortly before his
speech, he was brought out from the auditors' box to
sit on a bench all by himself, just by the Secretary's
pulpit and alongside Maximos IV and his brethren.
For a minute he looked rather like a forlorn lay pseudo
eighth Patriarch, and I was relieved when Under-
Secretary Archbishop Krol of Philadelphia went to sit
with him whilst he waited his turn.

Let me quote Keegan's final sentence: "There is, by
wish of her Divine Founder, a distinction in the

Church between the hierarchy and the laity. But this distinction implies no distance. This debate in theCouncil has done much to bind us together inseparably in the single mission of the Church."

I suppose that he might have concluded with a fairly happy *"Dixi"*. Instead he said quite simply, "Thanks very much." The gratitude was mutual.

## 7. THE SIXTH WEEK

### *24th October 1964*

St Augustine often makes great play of numbers: if something has seven aspects it makes him think of the Sacraments; ten, the Commandments; three the Trinity, and so on. One wonders what he would have made of Schema 13 which has dominated the whole of this last week in the Council.

But there is certainly no mystic significance in the number 13 here. It just happens to have been the 13th item on the agenda for debate during this session. Perhaps it was because it was meant to have a different significance from all the other Council documentation that it was always known by its number rather than by its more formal title, "The Church in the World Today".

What is its background? Work originally started on it in January 1963, soon after the first session, when it was suggested that to counter the impression that the Council was concerned merely with theology and theory, an attempt should be made to show the Church's concern with the real problems facing mankind in the twentieth century. A mixed Commission, drawn from the Doctrinal Commission and the Lay

Apostolate Commission, was instructed to prepare a draft and this it did fairly comprehensively and inevitably at great length.

It was soon realized then that here was enough material for an entire Ecumenical Council and that it must be brought down to reasonable length. Eventually it was decided that a small Central Commission of six Bishops, with Bishop Guano of Livorno as Chairman and with the Redemptorist Father Häring as Secretary, should prepare a general Constitution on the role of the Church in the world; and that other matters should be dealt with in five annexes which would not actually come under discussion in the Council but would be there as a background guide for the Fathers.

In spite of great difficulties the Constitution was ready by last July to be sent out in advance to all the Bishops and the annexes were supplied about three weeks ago. These deal with the human person in society, marriage and the family, progress in culture, social and economic life, and peace and war; they are in fact a development of the main principles set out in the fourth and final chapter of the Constitution itself.

There was a noticeable air of excited anticipation in St Peter's last Tuesday when at last Bishop Guano introduced his brain-child. Personally, for his modesty and good humour, he is enormously popular and it was clear that on the whole the Fathers were most anxious that he should succeed.

But quite apart from these likable personal qualities, one must realize that the whole question of this document has been linked during the past weeks with the uncertainty about a fourth session. It is well known that several hierarchies as a whole had decided before coming to Rome in September to call for the total rejection of this document. The reasons given were devious. But after a while one noticed a growing apprehension lest if it were referred back for a complete re-write, such a task could not be completed by the end of this present session. Was there not a danger, so the argument ran, that if this were to happen the preparation of a new document would be put off to the non-existent "Greek kalends"? This led people to examine the document more precisely and gradually the tide began to swing. The main thing was to secure a fairly long debate on the document in general, pass it as a suitable basis for more detailed discussion chapter by chapter, and then press for its revision. I have little doubt that this was in the mind of most of the Fathers as they settled down to listen to Bishop Guano last Tuesday.

The Church could no longer maintain a closed-door policy, the Bishop said, "as if it were in a citadel, separated from others and intent on nothing else but defending its own values and its own members. Just as Christ came into the world and lived among us, sharing our humanity so that He might make us sharers in His divinity, so the Church recognizes herself living in the world, sharing in the life of men so that she may communicate to them the life of God. The Church is constituted of men and for men." The Bishop hoped that the text might become an efficacious instrument for the dialogue between the Church and the men of our time.

This question of just to whom the document is addressed is one which has blown up frequently during the past few days. It claims that it is addressed to all men of good will. But, it is pointed out, different men are likely to be moved by different arguments. Another oft-repeated criticism has been about the use of the word "world", sometimes with a territorial distinction and sometimes referring to what usually goes with the flesh and the devil. It also talks often of "the signs of the times", but even if this meant something to the Northern

Europeans, it left at least one Japanese Bishop saying he had not the least idea what it was talking about.

But in fact the debate started quietly enough. No one mentioned the Bomb or the Pill, though some expressed themselves dissatisfied with the inadequate treatment of the problems of married life. Cardinal Spellman, newly arrived from New York, said he thought the schema was admirable. Here was the Church addressing herself to all men in a manner that was simple, candid, humble and sincere. Cardinal Liénart, from France, gave it what was in fact a *iuxta modum*, calling for a number of clarifications. Cardinal Lercaro, from Italy, said that it would need a fourth session if the various difficulties in the document were to be dealt with adequately. The Canadian Cardinal Léger said that he thought it provided a sound basis for discussion, and Cardinal Döpfner, speaking for the German Bishops, said that there was room for improvement but it contained much that was good.

At this stage the only calls for its total rejection came from Cardinal Ruffini and Archbishop Morcillo of Madrid. The former said quite frankly that it contained a number of views that were wrong, that it stressed too much the limitation of the Church and made little mention of her immense contributions to mankind.

Wednesday brought a further spate of interventions, with Cardinal Suenens pointing out that the Church does not evangelize by civilizing, but civilizes by evangelizing. Cardinal Bea admitted that at first reading he thought the document was superficial. But further study had shown that it contained underlying principles which should perhaps be brought more clearly to the surface. And Archbishop Conway, Primate of All Ireland, pointed to a number of serious defects. He thought that it was timid in its approach to the world, he could not understand the omission of reference to such dangers as the commercialization of sex, and not enough was said about those regions where the Church is deprived of freedom.

So it moved on peacefully until Thursday morning. Everything had gone so quietly that it was almost with a sense of anticlimax that the Fathers assembled for the third day's debate. The explosion came with the first speech of the morning. The speaker was Westminster's Archbishop Heenan, whose interventions this session had never failed to arouse interest for their clarity of thought and diction. But on Thursday morning he delivered an oratorical masterpiece. The whole place was hushed when, after handing out the traditional praises for the efforts of the Commission, he went on to say that it was nevertheless quite obvious that the document they had presented was unworthy of a General Council of the Church.

Having spent such a long time on theological niceties, he said, the Council would become a laughing-stock in the eyes of the world if it were now to rush breathlessly through a debate on world hunger, nuclear war and family life. The world was awaiting from this Council wise advice on many grave problems. This document was going to dash their hopes. It read more like a sermon than a document of a Council.

Having delivered this broadside on the document itself, he next expressed horror at the thought that the annexes might be left so vague that the experts would be left to explain what the Bishops had meant. And he went on to take apart those few peripatetic *periti* who, without regard for the ordinary teaching authority of the Bishops, advanced their own theories, pouring scorn on what whole hierarchies taught.

This was strong stuff and the atmosphere was charged. The speech itself was punctuated with applause—and by laughter when, in polished rhetoric, he re-

E

ferred to the scholars who scarcely knew the world as it really is. "Certainly they are a simple as doves", he said, "but they are not always as wise as serpents."

But the intervention was not purely destructive. The Archbishop's main point was that the Commission lacked the technical advice to provide the Fathers with the facts which were a prerequisite for adequate judgment by the Council on such matters as contraceptive pills and nuclear weapons. He called for a completely new Commission which should include lay experts in bio-chemistry and nuclear physics. Let them set to work and produce the facts for discussion in a fourth and final session in a few years' time. By then some of the Episcopal College would have gone to their reward. "Perhaps", he added, "we shall then be able to help the Council more by our prayers than our speeches."

The Archbishop sat down to a greater round of applause than has been heard in St Peter's this session. But when the dust of oratory had settled, whilst there was widespread praise for his rhetoric, opinion remained divided. There were those who suggested that it took Archbishop Heenan to have the courage to say what many Fathers felt, and at the other extreme there were those who felt that the "*peritissimi*" had been hit too hard. But the debate was alive for the first time.

On Friday we reassembled ready for the counter-attack. But on the whole it was a fairly gentle affair. The Benedictine Abbot Reetz from Germany playfully expressed fear about speaking at all in view of the sheltered life he had apparently led. Perhaps the forty monks once sent to make angels of the English people did not really know the world. He claimed with spirit that the monasteries also had contact with the world today, although some of the wags suggested afterwards that there was little in the subsequent speech in proof of this contention. But just after 11 o'clock the Moderators called for a halt and Bishop Guano was given the chance to answer various points before the vote was taken. Many valuable observations had been made. Certain lay experts had already been consulted and more experts would be heard. Significantly he added that the Commission had hesitated to go too deeply into points of a delicate nature, and the Pope had already announced that a study of these matters was being carried out by competent biologists and sociologists and had reserved judgment to himself. There need be no anxiety about the time element. He was authorized to say that there would be a fourth session.

There it was. The Fathers must vote as to whether to accept this document as a basis for discussion chapter by chapter. One hour later the result was announced. 1579 ayes, 296 noes. The "Save Schema 13 Movement" was in the clear, and next week we go on to discuss its contents in greater detail.

# 8. THE SEVENTH WEEK

## *31st October 1964*

ARE YOU one of those folk who regard 13 as an unlucky number? Or, to be cussed, do you think it lucky? Dismiss it as nonsense, of course, but remember that it all goes back to the Middle Ages when the number 13 had an almost holy meaning. It was meant to remind you of Our Lord and the 12 Apostles, and so people did things together in thirteens, went on pilgrimage in groups of 13 and so on. Came the troubles and the Protestant reformers swept away such nonsense with other superstitions. The number 13 became definitely unholy, unlucky if you like. Try to seat 13 people at a table even today and you'll see what I mean.

But not at all tables. On two mornings this week in St Peter's the Mass preceding the day's business has been a concelebration—with a presiding celebrant and 12 others. Back to the holy 13 again, to the Last Supper and the first Eucharist.

Wednesday was the sixth anniversary of the election of good Pope John. And that called for something special. It was also the anniversary of the ordination and episcopal consecration of the Council's General Secretary, Archbishop Felici; so he concelebrated with twelve of the parish priests now admitted to the Council. Next day was an even more remarkable occasion, being the priestly Silver Jubilee of one of the Moderators, Cardinal Döpfner of Munich. So he also presided at a concelebration and with him twelve of the Fathers keeping their Silver Jubilees as bishops. What a lot has happened since that day in 1939 when Joseph Kiwanuka of Uganda became the first African bishop in modern times—just as Julius Döpfner was being ordained a priest.

There was the holy meaning of 13. But if you were to go up to one of the Fathers and say smartly to him, "What does 13 make you think of?" it is the Boston treasury to a cassock button that he'd reply, "Schema 13, The Church in the World Today." For that's what's been on his mind all this past week, and most of the week before, and it is likely to be there for several days to come.

Last Monday morning a start was made with the Introduction and Chapter 1—on the now famous Signs of the Times, and on Man's Vocation, seen from spiritual and temporal aspects. This double viewpoint is half the trouble, as Bishop De Roo of Canada pointed out. It is most important to warn the faithful, he said, against positing a dichotomy—definitely an O.K. word in the Council, this—between the natural and supernatural roles in their vocation. Just as Christ became flesh to redeem the world from within, so man's vocation should be seen as his incarnation into the world and all its problems.

Chapters 2 (on the Church dedicated to the service of man) and 3 (on how Christians should behave in the world) brought more speakers, though not a lot more life to the debate. Bishop Morrow from India aroused interest by claiming not to speak in the name of umpteen bishops, as is now the vogue, but in the name of many millions of the Church's sons and daughters in the world. They were puzzled, he said. They could see no proportion between the Church's precepts and God's commandments. Would God really condemn to eternal punishment the man eating meat on Friday in the same way as the adulterer and the murderer? The religion of Christ is that of love and no precept should lightly be imposed under pain of mortal sin.

Monsignor Cule of Mostar, the Jugoslav Bishop who put the name of Joseph into the Canon of the Mass, made a point of great power when one recalls his spell in a Communist jail. The Church works in the world, he said, but she doesn't seek temporal dominion, so the State has nothing to fear from her. Her role is to give to the State principles of Christian morality and the Divine Law. She does not enter the political arena and she asks no privilege other than her freedom.

Monday and Tuesday brought many references to world poverty. Many extolled the spirit of poverty, though some were left asking whether poverty in spirit was something which the really poor were able to recognize. Archbishop Golland of Brazil took the General Secretary up on one of his more extravagant forms of address: he sometimes refers to the Fathers of the Council as *"Patres ornatissimi"*. The Brazilian Archbishop reckoned that coloured silks and gorgeous lace separated a Bishop from the man in the street and he hoped that all the Fathers would be wearing black cassocks for the fourth session, whenever that might be.

Many other points came up, not least the alleged separation of the Church from the vital world of modern science. But, let's face it, most of the Bishops were waiting for Chapter 4, the one dealing with the real problems facing mankind today.

But first came an announcement from the Moderator. Certain matters clearly could not be discussed in detail in St Peter's. The Fathers would exercise discretion and could send in their written views on any matter of which they could not treat in public debate. Bishop Wright of Pittsburgh followed for the Commission which had prepared the schema. He explained that whilst the Church wished to express her mind on the main problems of the day, she could not be expected always to give a quick and ready answer and she could not attempt to deal with all questions. He repeated Bishop Guano's assurance to Archbishop Heenån that the Commission had the help of competent experts, clerical and lay, though as yet no names have been given. The Fathers should be patient and not expect too much too soon. The Chapter would be dealt with section by section.

The first section dealt with the dignity of the human person, and perhaps the most interesting point made here came from Archbishop O'Boyle of Washington, speaking in the name of the U.S. Bishops. He called for a special section dealing with racial discrimination. Racism existed in many forms in many parts of the world, but it was everywhere a moral and religious problem, and this Chapter should state clearly the theological, not political, grounds for its condemnation.

And still we waited for the heart of the matter: Section 21 dealing with the dignity of marriage and the family.

This time it was Archbishop Dearden of Detroit who spoke for the Commission. Christian parents, collaborating with God in raising a family, could make up their own minds about the number of their children. Their judgment would be formulated under the influence of true love and under the guidance of their conscience. But any methods they might use to regulate the size of their family had to be judged according to the teaching and mind of the Church. Nothing could be permitted which was opposed to the natural orientation of the marital act. The schema had purposely avoided the question of the different brands of pill and the Holy Father had reserved this question to himself as it would certainly not be resolved in the Aula of St Peter's.

I think everyone wondered how far the limitations of public debate would restrict an adequate discussion of this subject. In fact it had the effect of lifting the whole discussion from the question of this pill, or that device, to the question of the primary end of marriage and of contraception itself. As was to be expected, Cardinal Ruffini insisted that the general directives of *Casti Connubii* be incorporated in this text, and then came three sledge-hammer blows calling into question the Church's traditional thinking on marriage.

First, Cardinal Léger of Montreal. The Church had found no answer to the grave problems of married people, he claimed. Many theologians believed that the fundamental purpose of marriage must be examined, that present difficulties arose from an inadequate understanding of the ends of marriage. In addition to the procreation of children, human conjugal love, involving soul and body, should be put forward as a true end of marriage. The Council should present both these ends of marriage as good and holy in themselves.

Cardinal Suenens followed with a plea for courage in facing up to this objective study of the theology of marriage. No one was trying to modify the traditional doctrine of the Church. The Gospel does not change. But perhaps the text "increase and multiply" had been emphasized to the neglect of "they shall be two in one flesh". The Commission must determine whether our classic doctrine took sufficient account of modern findings in the field of biology and psychology. Their findings must be submitted to the supreme *magisterium* and the names of these lay experts should be published. And then came Maximos IV, Patriarch of Antioch, appealing to the Council Fathers to open their eyes to a situation which led many of the faithful to live apart from the laws of the Church.

On Friday the "ding-dong" continued. Cardinal Alfrink welcomed the Commission of Inquiry. Only when genuine certitude was reached about the content of divine law could the Church bind or release the consciences of the faithful.

Cardinal Ottaviani next presented himself as the eleventh of twelve children of a working man and he was unwilling to accept the contention that married couples could determine the number of children they ought to have. We could not escape the fact that these new theories must give rise to the belief that the Church had erred in her teaching on matrimony—teaching subsequently set forth for the Fathers by the Irish Dominican, Cardinal Browne.

Bishop Hervas of Spain, speaking for 126 Fathers of different nationalities, argued that the approach of the schema was too negative, scarcely a Christian pronouncement at all. We should be praising those parents who thankfully accepted the children God gave them and we should be realistically encouraging financial relief and benefits to ease the burden of large families.

Just how complex the whole issue was when treated universally emerged from Archbishop Yago of the

Ivory Coast, where the problems of marriage are polygamy, lack of free consent from the women and the demand for excessive dowries.

At this point the Moderators called a halt. It was a quarter to twelve on a Friday morning and one of these days I must count up how often a closure motion has been moved successfully in the last hour of the last day of the week. And there it was. All over? I doubt it. There was still a long list of uncalled speakers.

The last moments of the week were devoted to a consideration of culture, a nice subject for the Fathers to brood over these next days. But the weekend began well. I am glad to report that Abbot Reetz of Germany, who last week taunted Archbishop Heenan about Augustine and the angels, buried the monastic hatchet yesterday and at the Archbishop's invitation lunched with the angels at the English College: and all unknown to an omniscient Press.

## 9. THE EIGHTH WEEK

### 7th November 1964

I HAVE already attempted to explain the rather complicated debating system of the Vatican Council in terms of British Parliamentary procedure. This week in the Council we have seen the use of a measure by no means unknown in the Mother of Parliaments, especially when there is a lot of business on hand: what we call here in Rome the closure motion, and is usually known at Westminster as the guillotine. Strange as it may seem, the closure motion is not a piece of machinery widely known on the continent of Europe, and when the daily Congregations began in St Peter's in 1962 there was no provision for its use. It was only after weeks of repetitious interventions on the early chapters of the original schema on the Liturgy that it was recognized that something must be done if the work of the Council was ever to bear fruit. You remember, it was the time when Cardinal Cushing returned to Boston and told the Press: "I give the Council another 200 years." At that rate of progress his calculation was not far out. And it was largely due to a proposal put forward by the English Bishops that a regulation was approved whereby the Commission of Presidents—the "12 Apostles" as they were known—was empowered to seek the views of the Fathers when they thought that enough had been said on any one subject. A two-thirds majority, indicated by standing vote, was sufficient to call discussion on that topic to a halt.

In that first session this device was employed on only about three occasions and never unsuccessfully. In the second session, the power of moving the closure was transferred to the newly-appointed Moderators, known suitably enough as the "4 Evangelists". Even then, in the interests of free discussion it was used but sparingly.

This time it has been a regular feature of the session, employed with increasing frequency and, so far as I can recall, always successfully. The Moderators have shown great skill in the timing of its use, and now that the Fathers are faced with an immense amount of business if a number of Constitutions is to be ready by the end of this session in a fortnight's time, the Fathers are being called to their feet several times each week.

The irony of it all is that the original proponents of the closure motion, the English Fathers, have been prominent amongst the recent casualties. In the great debate on marriage and the family, Bishop Pearson and Bishop Holland were only two speeches away from the microphone when the closure came. On Wednesday last Bishop Holland had the same frustrating experience. On Thursday Bishop Wheeler was separated from the microphone by only one speaker when the guillotine fell and we lost his intervention on the social and economic order. At the end of that same morning, Father Mahon, the Superior General of the Mill Hill Fathers, was at the top of the list of those still wanting to speak on world poverty. Just how unlucky can you be? And now speeches are being restricted to those whose interventions have the support of seventy of the Fathers: which is quite a predicament for those who submitted their texts nearly a month ago before this measure was announced. And it presents special problems for members of relatively small hierarchies.

Still, with a growing understanding of collegiality we listened to others talking last Wednesday on that part of Schema 13 which deals with culture. Here Cardinal Lercaro found himself on the wrong side of the Moderators' table when he was gonged by Cardinal Döpfner for overrunning his time. But it was a good speech. The Church must be cautious, the Cardinal said, in relying on past cultural riches of theological and philosophical systems. She must avoid outmoded scientific language which is unintelliglbe to the world today and she must boldly show herself open to contemporary culture. He would like to see less reliance on ecclesiastical academies and more theologian-bishops.

Bishop Carli, on the other hand, wanted pride of place given to philosophy, history, literature and—he raised a laugh here—law, even though the word "juridical" had been almost a term of abuse in this Council. A more pragmatic approach came from Bishop Proano of Ecuador, who spoke of the need for basic education in Latin America, of whose two hundred million inhabitants, eighty million were unable to read or write.

So we passed on to the next section dealing with the social and economic order, and here again there were some hard facts given about the situation in Latin America. Bishop Benitez of Paraguay pointed out that one-third of the present Catholic world lives in South America and, at the present rate of increase, by the year 2000 it will constitute almost half of the Church. The population explosion has brought profound economic changes and the Church as a whole must make a concerted drive to ensure that the reforms set forth in *Mater et Magistra* be applied throughout Latin America.

All this made a good preparation for the consideration of Section 24 dealing with world poverty. The task of introducing this discussion was entrusted to the American lay auditor, Mr James Norris, well known for his outstanding work in the field of international relief. Jim Norris said that it was on the instructions of Archbishop Felici that he read his *Relatio* in Latin and he played one back at the Archbishop, so given to the use of superlatives, by referring to him as the *"Amabilissimus (sic) Secretarius Generalis"*. In his speech he gave a telling picture of the uneven distribution of the world's goods. He told of a Bishop who had said to him, "My people live not only in poverty but in permanent misery". Poverty meant that for millions of people expectancy of life was no more than thirty-five years. "From this Ecumenical Council", he said, "should come a clarion call for action which would involve the creation of a structure that would devise the kind of institutions, contacts, forms of co-operation and policy, which the Church can adopt to secure full Catholic participation in the world-wide attack on poverty."

He was followed by Cardinal Frings who set forth a succession of practical proposals largely based on the experience of German Catholics in their magnificent

*Misereor* Foundation. Something of this kind should be set up in every country by Episcopal Conferences to alleviate poverty in their own and in other more needy territories. And the work should be co-ordinated with a view to collaboration with international organizations such as the United Nations and F.A.O. No one who attended last Thursday's debate can have failed to be moved by the urgency of the situation and by the practical possibilities of being able to do something about it.

Events took a new turn on Friday when, to the delight of the Fathers, His Holiness the Pope attended Mass in St Peter's celebrated in the Ethiopian Rite and then, after the Gospels had been enthroned to an accompaniment of hand-bells and tom-toms, stayed on to inaugurate the debate on the Missionary activity of the Church.

The very title of this subject in indicative. No longer is it desired that one should think of the Foreign Missions as some distant and extra-mural department of the Church. The Church's Mission is one, and if collegiality has any meaning, concern for the work in what are called missionary territories must be shared by all.

But collegiality was exemplified in a very special way when the Holy Father took his place in the centre of the long table with the Cardinal Presidents. Here, amidst his brother Bishops, the Vicar of Christ addressed his brethren. He said that he had chosen that day on which to be present in order to indicate the importance he attached to this discussion on the missions. "We, the successor of Peter," he said, "and you, the successors of the Apostles, have been divinely commanded to go into the whole world, preaching the Gospel to every creature that the world may be saved." He stayed in the Aula whilst Cardinal **Agagianian** moved the formal introduction of this document and, obviously moved, spoke of the Holy Father's forthcoming visit to India *"qualis et quantus missionarius"*.

This debate on the Missions started calmly enough. Cardinal Rugambwa stressed the need of adaptation in mission lands. Successful missionaries had baptized native values. A failure to put off western appearances led to confusion with colonialism.

But this Saturday morning the Mission Fathers came out into the open and called for the rejection of these propositions as being totally inadequate. Bishop Lamont of Rhodesia in a flood of rhetoric tore the document into oratorical shreds and scattered the bits to the four winds of change. He wanted a real schema and my bet is that when this vote is taken on Monday he will get it.

There, with only a fortnight to run, we must end for this week. Vote upon vote has been taken these last days as the document on the Pastoral Duty of Bishops approaches its final form.

One last point. This morning Cardinal Suenens, claiming like so many others to be speaking for countless African bishops, took the occasion of his intervention on the Missions to make a personal statement about his earlier speech on contraception. He denied hotly that he had called for the rejection of the Church's traditional doctrine. He merely wanted all modern knowledge and teaching synthesized and submitted to the supreme *magisterium* of the Pope. So, political, medical, theological and conciliar correspondents, please note.

## 10. THE NINTH WEEK

### *14th November 1964*

INTERNATIONAL conferences nearly always follow the same pattern. There is an initial period when speeches are made and positions adopted; then comes a moment of crisis: after which the conference either breaks down or else it moves rapidly to agreement—perhaps by way of compromise—and so to conclusion.

The sessions of the Second Vatican Council have proved no exception to this rule. There have been moments of crisis and when these have been resolved and the closing date has come into sight, things have developed a certain "holy speed" to ensure that as much of the agenda as possible has been covered by the target date.

Certainly that was true of the first two sessions. But this third session has moved at such a rapid rate throughout that these last days have seen the Fathers trying to deal with important items at a quite unprecedented rate. Let's face it: almost everyone is now dead tired, and instead of merely keeping abreast with what has been called "the caravan of God", one has now to watch out lest one is metaphorically bowled over by a hurtling Conciliar juggernaut.

Another feature of the last weeks of each session has always been fluctuating rumours as to the progress of the various Commissions struggling to batter their material into final form so that the Pope may have Constitutions and Decrees ready for promulgation by the close of the session. This past week has run according to pattern: on Monday it was rumoured that no Constitutions at all would be ready by the end of the session. By Tuesday night we were reliably assured that as many as four documents would be complete and

passed through all stages of Conciliar procedure: the
Church, the Eastern Churches, Ecumenism and perhaps even the Declaration on Religious Liberty. So
it swung back and forth. The theologians and the
organization men worked by day and a great deal of
the night. This morning the Fathers were issued with
the *modi* for the remaining chapters of *De Ecclesia*
and we knew that all was well.

Meantime this week in the Council has seen a whole
series of votes and speeches on no less than four separate
schemata. When the "House" rose last Saturday, the
missionary activity of the Church was under discussion
and we picked up again with this subject on Monday
morning—incidentally quite one of the wettest mornings on which the buses have had to decant their
episcopal cargoes into the Piazza. But the rain had done
nothing to quench the zeal with which one bishop after
another called for the rejection of the propositions set
before them. The outcome was inevitable; it was just a
matter of time and after six more speeches the guillotine
fell. But not before the well-known tones of Bishop
Fulton Sheen had silenced the entire Aula. With hushed
voice, suited perhaps to the single viewer glued to the
"goggle-box", he undoubtedly commanded the attention of over two thousand individuals in St Peter's. The
poverty of the Missions was his theme: as chastity had
been the product of Trent, and obedience that of
Vatican I, let poverty be the fruit of Vatican II. Just as
only a wounded Christ convinced a doubting Thomas,
so also a poor Church would convince an unbelieving
world. It was a skilful performance and we all hung on
his words. "Ah", said a French *peritus* near me, "la
technique!"

The Commission responsible for the document anti-
cipated the verdict and with diplomatic subtlety
proposed the withdrawal of the propositions for re-

writing as a schema to be discussed in the fourth session. Their proposal was endorsed by 1601 votes to 311.

Then back to Schema 13, to where we had broken off at the end of Thursday morning, the article dealing with World Poverty. Here the luck of the English turned: Father Mahon, the Superior General of the Mill Hill Fathers, caught the Moderators' eye and delivered an intervention he had held in cold storage over the weekend. The central problem of our age, said Father Mahon, was that the world was divided into "haves" who virtually want for nothing, and "have-nots" who lack almost everything. The Church must speak out boldly or her claim to have dialogue with the world would not be taken seriously. After the lengthy treatment given by the Council to ecclesiastical matters, some striking action by the Church was necessary to show that she was deeply involved in man's struggle to stay alive, and not merely trying to save disembodied souls.

I doubt if even Father Mahon was prepared for the striking action by the Church which followed on Friday morning. His Holiness the Pope had obviously gauged the depths of the feelings of the Fathers and after a prolonged concelebration in the Byzantine Rite by His Beatitude Maximos IV and his Oriental brethren, Archbishop Felici announced that the Holy Father had decided to give his papal tiara to the poor. Quite simply Pope Paul rose and taking his silver tiara—given to him by the people of Milan at the time of his coronation— placed it on the altar. A symbolic gesture? Certainly. There is nothing more symbolic he could have given away—something his own, and something of immense consequence. Its precise value and its ultimate destination are not important. In the footsteps of his Master, the Vicar of Christ was pledging the Church as the mother of the poor.

F

From poverty to peace and war. And discussion of the last article of Schema 13 showed not so much division of opinion amongst the Fathers as the complexity of the whole problem of modern armaments. There were frequent references to Pope John's famous encyclical *Pacem in Terris*, and Cardinal Alfrink pointed out that if the Council was merely to condemn the use of uncontrollable weapons, it might appear that she excluded from such strictures the use of the "clean" bomb. Bishop Ancel pleaded that the good of the human family today required all nations to renounce the right to war, retaining only those arms necessary to preserve internal order. He would like to see an international force given the means to suppress war.

But on Tuesday Bishop Hannan of Washington recalled the moral principles of a just defensive war. It was ridiculous for the Council to pretend that it did not know the source of aggression. To have dialogue with atheistic materialists we must have liberty. We should praise those who defend freedom, especially those who die for it.

This point was taken up by Archbishop Beck of Liverpool. The Council should express sympathy, he said, with those who hold the heavy burden of responsibility for the use of nuclear weapons. The government of a country had a grave duty to protect its citizens and under certain circumstances it might be true that peace could only be pursued by retention of weapons as a deterrent against unjust aggression. He also made the nice point that there might well exist legitimate targets for even immensely powerful nuclear weapons, instancing ballistic or satellite missiles in outer space. Therefore a universal condemnation of nuclear weapons could not be sustained.

Of course all agreed on the desirability of disarmament, balanced and simultaneous if possible, but unilateralism also had its exponents. At the end of the day Bishop Guano closed the debate. The discussions had been invaluable, he said. He hoped that before the end of the session some propositions could be presented to the Fathers as test votes on the general orientation of the Council's thought so as to guide the Commission when the revision of Schema 13 was undertaken.

Next, from the bomb to the religious life, which occupied discussion all of Wednesday and most of Thursday—not unreasonable when one remembers that about a third of the Bishops are in fact religious. Cardinal Döpfner did not think the propositions adequate. They should stress not only a spiritual renewal but also the accommodation of religious life to the needs of our time. This was a recurrent theme with speakers, some wanting more emphasis on the contemplative life, others wanting monks and nuns to come out of their enclosures and to come to grips with the problems of the world.

Cardinal Suenens developed this theme. Nuns should be treated as adults, enjoying the freedom needed for apostolic action. Community rule should be adapted for this purpose and antiquated customs changed. Inevitably he hit the headlines again when he demanded that what he called "the distinctive but ridiculous garb of some congregations" should yield to the new look.

But the propositions as a block just made it, by 1,155 to 882 votes—though when taken separately today they were returned to the Commission with so many "modes" that they themselves are likely to have a new look when they come back into the Aula.

And it looks as though seminaries also are to have a new look, judging by the speeches on the next set of propositions, dealing this time with the training of priests. On Thursday we heard Archbishop Colombo of Milan arguing that Bishops should have the power to enable students to have a break in their course, if need be, for spiritual and other forms of development. We needed mature priests, with a full understanding of the nature and requirements of their office.

Today most of the big guns fired again. We had impassioned pleas from Cardinal Ruffini and Archbishop Staffa for the good name and teachings of St Thomas, though Cardinal Léger reminded them that there was more than one doctor of the Church. Cardinal Suenens pleaded for a practical, pastoral training to fit priests to help and work with the laity. And there was a well-balanced speech from Cardinal Döpfner, stressing the need for holy priests, equipped to meet contemporary needs. He also made the point that not all vocations must pass through a junior seminary, though for others a good home atmosphere was essential.

There is no doubt a tremendous last week lies ahead. We were warned this morning that there would probably have to be additional afternoon sessions to deal with all the voting. Vernacular reactions to this announcement were such that the General Secretary backed down a bit with *"Probabiliter"*. Certainly the Fathers need some time to study the present spate of new documents. And the Commissions need time for evening meetings as well. We shall see.

## 11. THE LAST WEEK

### *21st November 1964*

IT'S ALL over—for the time being, that is. This morning in a great ceremony in St Peter's His Holiness Pope Paul declared the third session of the Council formally at an end. Already a number of the Fathers are hurrying back to their dioceses. Rome's main line station has taken on the look which Paddington enjoys when the school children travel *home for* Christmas; and Fiumicino Airport is cluttered up with clerics wearing suits and trilby hats for the first time in ten weeks. Tomorrow will see the last of us moving out, and Rome will settle down once more to an inter-session breather.

What a climax this last week has been. We knew it was going to be tough and we had been warned that afternoon sessions might prove necessary. But on Monday it was announced that this threat would not be carried through, though merely because the Fathers would need the time to study the flood of new documents upon which votes have had to be cast. And we were warned that we might have to be kept in school until 1 o'clock each day if we did not get a move on.

But we had better go back to Monday, when the Council Fathers were still debating the important question of seminary training. There had been a great deal of advance criticism of the inadequacy of the original propositions on this subject, and the Commission had done a good job of anticipation by revising them before the debate commenced. These revised propositions proved far more satisfactory and the generally expected "send them back" treatment did not come.

Last Saturday a reminder was given by Cardinal Léger that St Thomas was not the only Doctor of the Church. On Monday it was Cardinal Bacci who made the comeback. He said that if anyone dared to belittle the teaching of St Thomas it would be the same as daring to put the Council not only above the Pope, but almost against the Pope—which none of the Fathers would ever think of doing. Here was a bit of a dig and most of the Fathers did not like it.

Later that morning we heard from Bishop Schmitt of

Metz who recommended that, because of the artificial
life of a seminary, students should have a period of pro-
bationary ministry in a parish under the direction of an
experienced parish priest. But Bishop Charue of Namur
stressed that we should not lose sight of spiritual goods
just at the price of trying to instil a preoccupation with
efficiency.

Tuesday saw a continuation of this debate and much
attention was given to the last speech on the subject by
Bishop Reuss from Germany, who asked that a fuller
treatment be given of the positive view of celibacy, lest
it be seen principally as a renunciation, an unwelcome
*sine qua non* for the priesthood.

The debate on this subject was closed by a speech
from a parish priest, one of several who have been
admitted to the Aula in a representative capacity
during the past weeks. The vote on the propositions
then revealed the extent to which its protagonists had
succeeded, for only 41 out of 2117 votes were shown to
be *non placet*.

During the morning a number of other important
votes were taken, including one dealing with those parts
of the Constitution *De Ecclesia* which deal with
collegiality. The announcement of an overwhelming
majority in favour was greeted with enthusiastic
applause. There has been great praise these last days
for the *periti* of the Doctrinal Commission and for no
one more than the Belgian Monsignor Philips who has
led a devoted team of theologians in the constant work
of revision. There has also been praise of a certain
explanatory note, said to have been inserted at the wish
of the Holy Father himself. Its importance in clarifying
the notion of collegiality is now fully recognized.

The last hours of Tuesday were given over to the
question of Christian Education—*De Scholis* as it
was originally called. Archbishop Beck of Liverpool ex-

pressed his regret that the title had been changed. The Archbishop was speaking for a very large number of bishops from the Commonwealth and he made on his pet subject quite his best intervention to date. His main concern was with the rights of all parents to educate their children according to their consciences. He pointed out that as Catholic parents paid their rates and taxes like their fellow citizens, their rights deserved recognition by the public authorities. This led him to suggest that gratitude be expressed to those governments which recognized the value of Christian education by giving financial assistance to Catholic schools. And he closed with a well-deserved tribute to Catholic teachers upon whom the efficacy of Christian education ultimately depends.

But it was Thursday, when the debate on education gave way to a discussion of the Sacrament of Matrimony, which saw events that pushed the Council right back into the headlines of the newspapers of the world. The discussion of Matrimony formed little more than background music, for the trouble blew up about that thorny question of Religious Liberty. You remember that it came up for discussion a year ago and there was widespread disappointment when at the end of the second session the document was not put to a vote because there was no time. Last September saw it back again, though cast in rather different form, and after the debate it went back to the Secretariat for Christian Unity, charged with its revision in the light of opinions expressed at that time.

For some time now there have been those strange Roman rumours about strange Roman happenings which always seem to add up to delay. It seems that the revision was completed by the third week in October, but the fact remains that it did not come back to the Fathers until Tuesday last. It was said that the delays had been occasioned because the works of the Vatican printing press were almost gummed up with Conciliar documentation. But a number of the Fathers, claiming that its revision was so widespread that it almost constituted a new document, approached the Presidents with the complaint that, with all the other papers to be worked through, they had not time to give adequate consideration to Religious Liberty. And so on Wednesday it was announced that a vote would be taken the following day to see how widespread were these misgivings. The Fathers would vote, therefore, on the straight issue of whether they wanted to vote at once on the terms of the document itself.

Came Thursday morning, however, and the Dean of the Presidents, Cardinal Tisserant, announced what appeared to be a change of mind, though no further reasons were given. The document would be formally introduced into the Aula, and written views could be sent in. But no vote would take place until the next session. At this the atmosphere became electric. The American Bishops have always attached the greatest importance to this document, and within moments the Council chamber half emptied and the lobbies were full of Bishops queuing to add their names to a rapidly prepared petition that at least some preliminary vote should be taken.

Meantime it fell to Bishop De Smedt, one of the great orators in the Church today, to read the *Relatio*, and he rose to the occasion as did his voice, trembling at times with emotion as he presented the document which, after all, was not be to voted upon. As he reached his climax the Bishops poured back into the Aula from the transepts, pressing about the Presidential table in much the same way as M.P.s crowd behind the Speaker's chair at moments of crisis in the House of Commons.

The Bishop regained control of his voice and with superb dignity monotoned the chronicle of events in the history of this unhappy business. "Let us pray", he concluded, "to the Holy Spirit that He may illumine our minds at this moment." Almost unprecedented applause greeted his conclusion. At first it seemed a spontaneous reaction to a masterpiece of oratory. But no sooner had the applause begun to die down, than a second wave began and one recognized now that here was a determined attempt by a number of the Fathers to show their desire to pass the declaration by acclamation.

To no avail. Within less than an hour over 800 signatures had been gathered and the petitions were brought to an obviously distressed Cardinal Meyer who gathered them under his arm and in company with Cardinal Ritter and Cardinal Léger walked steadily across St Peter's to convey the views of the signatories to the Pope.

The decision was made known on Friday and was clearly reached on a strictly juridical basis. The Presidents had been approached by a number of the Fathers with what had seemed to be a reasonable request. In making its decision the Presidency had not exceeded the powers conferred upon it in the *regolamento*. Its decision was therefore upheld, though the assurance was given that if possible the declaration on Religious Liberty would have priority on the Agenda for the next Session.

Whilst Press reports of a "punch-up" in St Peter's are obviously grossly exaggerated, one need not disguise that this has been an unhappy business, the more unhappy in that it has come at the end of a really superb session of work in the Council. As an American Bishop said to me, in the best rugby football parlance: "The trouble is that every time the ball comes out of the scrum somebody hoofs it back."

Is it to be wondered that the last two days of discussion on the Sacrament of Matrimony received scant attention? There was a particularly impressive speech from Archbishop Krol of Philadelphia, and Archbishop Heenan, to whom fell the task of offering Mass on the last morning congregation of the session, spoke also of his pleasure at the proposed relaxation of rules regarding the ceremonial to be followed at mixed marriages.

But at the end of Friday morning it was clear that no detailed vote on this document was practical and it was agreed by a two-thirds majority to transmit the proposals to the Sovereign Pontiff for appropriate action.

And there we were. Votes of thanks were passed in all directions and we made ready for the solemn public ceremonies for the closure.

It was just after 9 this morning when Pope Paul entered St Peter's in a solemn procession from which only the bearer of a tiara was missing. His Holiness was accompanied by his concelebrants for the Mass, some twenty-four bishops of dioceses containing major shrines of Our Lady. Lourdes was there, and Quito; the Archbishop of Tuam for Knock and our own Bishop Parker of Northampton for Walsingham—what a fitting reward for this golden jubilarian who has not missed a single Daily Congregation throughout the three sessions.

The Concelebration of Mass was as moving as ever, as was the sight of the lay Auditors coming forward to receive Communion from the Pope. Then the Gospel Book was enthroned, the *Adsumus* prayer recited and His Holiness intoned the *Veni Creator*.

At ten to eleven Archbishop Felici went to his pulpit to begin the reading of the wonderful new Constitution on the Church. There was no time for more than representative paragraphs and then the whole was submitted to formal vote by the Fathers. Half an hour later the result was declared: 2151 in favour and only 5 dissentients. Here was one of the great fruits of the Council and soon two more Constitutions had been added—those on the Eastern Churches and on Ecumenism.

Historic and moving moments these—especially for the Observers from other faiths who have sat so long and patiently through all the debates: a fact remarked on by His Holiness in his Address which followed.

I cannot hope to do more than single out a few points from the Pope's speech. He expressed happiness especially at the Constitution on the Church, saying that after the fourth and final session—no date given as yet—he would regularly convoke some members of the episcopate for consultation and would welcome their views on such matters as the reorganization of the Curia. This was clearly a reference to the oft-advocated Senate of Bishops.

Much of the Address was devoted to Our Lady, whose feast day it is today, and whom he proclaimed Mother of the Church, of the People of God. To her he confided the whole human race, imploring her to bring all men to the knowledge of her Divine Son.

Just before one o'clock I made my way out into the Piazza. The searing heat of September's opening session had gone, but all the hopes expressed that day by the Pope, that the nature of the Church might be clearly defined in this session, have been wonderfully fulfilled. Yes, today is history all right: Church history, but the history of the Church in the Modern World. And back to that modern world the Fathers are fast returning. "See you next year?" Current rumours are of an eight week session in June or September. Presumably no decision will be taken until it is clear as to how long it will take the Commissions to do their home-work. Which is almost where we came in.

# III. INTERVENTIONS

# 1. THE PASTORAL CARE OF SOULS

*Intervention of the Right Reverend Brian Foley, Bishop of Lancaster, in the Debate "De Cura Animarum", 18th September 1964*

THERE IS one thing that I would like briefly to speak about, namely the necessity of the subject of the "Care of Souls" being given a greater part and greater emphasis in this schema—or better still its being given a separate schema.

In the last analysis the purpose of this Council is a *pastoral* one; it is concerned particularly with the restoring of religious practice in parts of the world now "dechristianized" and with the apostolate to those who have not yet received the faith. Now such a restoration of religious life will come not only—not even primarily—by a new liturgy, by new doctrinal and scriptural interpretations, but rather by a restoring of truly pastoral practice in our parishes by parish priests and their assistants. This is shown by the history of the Church and by present experience.

There was in former days, as can be seen in various written works, an intense pastoral apostolate, that is to say, intimate contact between priest and people. We read of the splendour of the pastoral life in such works as the Italian book *Promessi Sposi*, for instance, where the figures of Fra Cristofero and of Cardinal Federigo and so many others are shown. These were indeed great pastoral priests who like their Master gave themselves to their people *conversando cum hominibus*. There was little neglect of religious practice in those days where priests and people were so intimately in contact.

Present experience teaches us the same. Where there exists a close contact between priest and people, speaking generally, there will be found a vigorous religious life; where it is lacking, the churches are empty.

Our Divine Lord by his words and example inculcated the need of personal contact between priest and people. On the other hand, he said little concerning worship and matters of speculative doctrine.

What is so worrying today is that it is being taken for granted in so many places that such intimate personal contact between priest and people cannot be kept up. There appeared in an article in the *Osservatore Romano* during the month of July an account of a priest in a parish who had visited six hundred homes in his parish in a single year. This was written of as something unheard of and almost heroic; a book was written about it in which the priest was said to have brought back many to the Church, to have comforted many aged and sick, and so on.

Surely this is an extraordinary state of affairs. Is it not the strict duty of *every* priest working in parishes to be constantly, regularly and systematically visiting the homes of his people? How otherwise can he perform his apostolate? How can he be said to "know mine and mine know me"? How can he bring comfort to the aged and help those in distress; how will he bring back the lapsed without going to them in their homes?

If in some nations and regions there is still an intense religious practice, it is not because they have a more advanced liturgy, or great theological schools. It is because they have a truly pastoral clergy who faithfully perform their pastoral visitations and who know by name every least child in their parish or district. What good will it be if we succeed in cultivating a most advanced liturgy if our churches are empty? What good will it be if we develop a deep spirituality in an élite whilst the vast multitudes of our people do not even attend the Sunday Mass?

In my judgment there is a danger that this schema, and indeed this whole Council (which to date has been almost exclusively concerned with liturgical and speculatively doctrinal matters), by not sending forth to our priests the message that, first in importance, the Council regards a restoration of strict pastoral practice, will perpetuate the present widespread loss of priestly pastoral practice. In my opinion, it is essential to do so. The matter is of immense importance and will not wait.

I propose, therefore, that either there be prepared a new and separate schema "*De Cura Animarum*" or that a much greater part of this one on episcopal duties and office should be devoted to it. I would like to hear a debate upon such things as the following: the reasons why there has been such a falling away of urban populations; why religious practice is so high in some regions and so low in others; how *all* priests, even those whose work is primarily in diocesan offices, can be involved in some pastoral work in these times of such gravity. But there are so many things which ought to be discussed and investigated. I ask that ample place be allotted to them in our discussions here. Such a discussion would be most useful. Cities and countries all over the world are now similar in their conditions of life. It is therefore possible for experiences and lessons from one to be used in another. If we humbly and candidly set forth our experiences and problems, our failures and successes, we shall learn much that could be of value to God's Church in our own countries.

## 2. LIBERTY IN A PLURALIST SOCIETY

*Intervention of the Most Reverend John Carmel Heenan, Archbishop of Westminster, in the Debate on Religious Liberty, 28th September 1964*

I DARE to make a short intervention because the Hierarchy of England and Wales, many Bishops in Scotland, Ireland, Australia and New Zealand, as well as some of our neighbours in France and Belgium, think it opportune for me to tell the Fathers of the Council how the principles laid down in the Declaration on Religious Liberty have already been reduced to practice in our country.

It is well known that in England during the sixteenth century a bitter fight was joined between Protestants and Catholics. Religious liberty was soon banished from the land. The Blessed Martyrs of England and Wales by their death are witnesses to the ferocity of this persecution. To be honest, we must also confess that when the Catholic Queen Mary was on the throne, Protestants suffered a similar fate. By the end of the century the Protestants had triumphed and the Church of our forefathers had almost ceased to exist in Britain. The few who remained faithful to the Holy See were harassed and penalized. But persecution gradually relaxed and in the year 1828 Parliament passed the Catholic Emancipation Act freeing Catholics from most if not quite all of their civil disabilities.

Great Britain today can in no sense be described as Catholic. The Church of England is the Established Church and our Queen is its Head. It is true that many of our fellow citizens do not actively practise any religion. Most Englishmen would nevertheless call themselves Christians. Infants born in England are usually baptized, couples generally prefer to be married in church, and almost all who die are given Christian burial. There are also, of course, many who profess no religion of any kind.

There is a picture of a pluralist society in which, nevertheless, religion is honoured both publicly and in private. Although the Church of England is the Established Church, full religious liberty is granted to citizens of other faiths. Thus, for example, the State makes a substantial contribution for the provision of Church Schools and pays full salaries to their teachers, even to those who are priests, brothers or nuns. But—and this is the real point—precisely the same rights and privileges are granted to Catholic schools as to those belonging to the Church of England. It is clear to both Protestants and Catholics in England that liberty and equality of treatment for all is the only way of promoting peaceful relations among citizens.

That is why we praise and unreservedly approve the proposals in this schema on Religious Freedom. Pope Pius XII once said that the common good might impose a moral obligation in what are described as Catholic countries to respect the freedom of other religions. Today the world is small. What happens in one State can have consequences all over the world. For the sake of the common good, freedom of religion must flourish in every nation in the world.

Some fear the danger of allowing unrestricted scope to the propagation of error. These fears are real and not to be despised. No one can feel happy at the prospect of allowing the young or ignorant to be led into error. One of the great dangers of our time is contempt for all restraint. Liberty all too easily degenerates into lawlessness. Liberty nevertheless is precious. Despite all dangers it must be boldly defended.

If restrictions are to be applied, who is going to apply them? Only the State has the physical power to do so and all man's experience shows that the less the State interferes in religious matters the better. We are persuaded that the external practice of religion should be subject only to those restrictions which are absolutely necessary to safeguard public order.

The authors of this schema are to be praised for attempting to base it on something more positive than tolerance and the common good.

To bring this about patience, charity and firmness are needed in the practice of the Faith. Otherwise there is a danger of indifference.

It has been said in this debate that only the principles need be set down and that no attempt should be made to explain the underlying Catholic doctrine. This argument to me seems faulty. In a pastoral document of this kind it is necessary to give some indication of the methods by which we have reached our conclusions. This at least is certain that many outside the Church hold that Catholics do not sincerely believe in religious freedom. Let us declare to the whole world, once and for all, our heartfelt belief as Catholics in the full liberty of all the sons of God.

## 3. THE COUNCIL AND THE JEWS

*Intervention of the Most Reverend John Carmel Heenan, Archbishop of Westminster, in the Debate on "The Jews and Non-Christians", 29th September 1964*

IT IS not surprising that the Jews have received the new version of the Declaration "*De Judaeis*" without marked pleasure. The earlier pronouncement about the Jews in the schema on ecumenism was made public during the second session of the Council and in consequence its terms are well known to the Jews. It is natural that they should now be asking why certain changes have been made. It is impossible not to notice a subtle difference in the tone and spirit of the new version. In its present form the Declaration seems less forthcoming and less friendly. We of the Secretariat for Promoting Christian Unity prepared our text keeping in mind the hundreds of comments made between sessions by the Fathers of the Council. The wording of the document now in your hands is not precisely ours.

I have no idea which theologians were charged with drawing up the final draft of this Declaration. Let me say quite plainly that I have no suspicion of any kind that they set out to make our words less warm or our approach less generous. It is quite possible that these theologians have had little experience in ecumenical affairs. Such delicate material has to be handled with great care and even subtlety. This is especially true when dealing with the Jews whom frequent persecution has made particularly sensitive.

This sensitivity may well be the reason why the Jewish newspapers have complained so bitterly about the quotation from the Epistle of St Paul, to the Romans: "I would not have you ignorant, brethren, of this mystery . . . blindness has fallen upon a part of Israel but only until the tale of the Gentile nations is complete: then the whole of Israel will find salvation . . ." The Apostle of the Gentiles is here using what we call eschatological language. He is referring, in other words, to the end of the world when, it is hoped, all men, including the Jews, will return to the unity of the true people of God. I have no doubt in my own mind that this quotation was deliberately chosen as a proof of our brotherly love and desire for union with all the other sons of God. It is my view that the Jews are mistaken in regarding this text as a summons forthwith to give up their religion.

I must add, however, that the question of conversion, whether of individuals or of whole communities, really has no place in the context of ecumenism. The object of the Ecumenical Movement is to lead people of different religions to examine each other's beliefs. Neither party in the dialogue has any ambition to score victories. Its object is for all to grow in mutual understanding and esteem. That is why in discussing Christian Unity the schema made no mention of conversion either of the Orthodox in the East or of non-Catholics in the West. Our hope, nevertheless, of the return of all the brethren of Christ to the one fold remains strong. Our separated brethren pray no less earnestly than ourselves that led by the Holy Spirit all will eventually be united in one Church.

However good the intentions of those who inserted this quotation from St Paul's Epistle to the Romans, the fact is that it has been taken badly by the Jews. For me this is a sufficient reason for removing the quotation from the Declaration. Notice that in the same Declaration when talking about other non-Christian believers—such as the Moslems—no word is said about converting them. Here are the exact words of the text: "Although their opinions and doctrines differ from ours in many ways, nevertheless in many things they show a ray of that truth which enlightens every man coming into this world." But surely if these other non-Christian religions possess a ray of truth, the Jewish religion has much more since it is in a way the root of our own faith. Pope Pius XI once said: "We are all semites."

I want to end with a word about the famous question of deicide. In the earlier version of our Document the Jewish people was absolved from the crime of deicide. We must never forget that the text was published to the whole world. If, therefore, this absolution is deleted the interpretation will be made that the Fathers of the

Council, having had a year to think it over, now solemnly judge that the whole Jewish people, at least those alive at the time of Christ's death—are, in fact, guilty of the crime of deicide.

The Jews during this century have suffered grave and, indeed, inhuman injuries. In the name of Jesus Christ our Lord who from the cross forgave His executioners, I humbly plead that this Declaration of ours shall openly proclaim that the Jewish people *as such* is not guilty of the death of Our Lord. It would certainly be unjust in our own day if all the Christians of Europe were judged guilty of the death of millions of Jews in Germany and Poland. I maintain that it is no less unjust to condemn the whole Jewish people for the death of Christ.

## 4. HISTORICAL CHARACTER OF THE GOSPELS

*Intervention of the Right Reverend Christopher Butler, O.S.B., Abbot of Downside, in the Debate on "Divine Revelation", 6th October 1964*

THE PARAGRAPH of the present schema which deals with the historical character of the Gospels is a restrained and generally satisfactory statement. Everyone knows that anxieties have been felt in this field from two sides. Some fear that we are in process of losing the necessary historical foundation of our faith. Others want our scholars to have all rightful liberty in pursuing their task which is of such great service to the Church.

I wish to say something more about this liberty. The question of the historical value of the Gospels can be looked at from two angles. From the point of view of faith, there is no doubt that the Gospels, along with the other books of the Bible, are inspired—with all the consequences deriving from that dogma. It is however certain that the notion of "literary types" is applicable to the Gospels as it is to the other inspired books. Who would question that many difficulties in the Old Testament have been solved by the application of this notion, without detriment to the faith? And by means of it apparent contradictions between the Bible and other ascertained truths, of natural science or history, have been removed. Neither faith nor defined doctrine precludes the same process from application to the Gospels.

The historicity of the Gospels can also be looked at from the point of view of an *approach* to faith—what is called the point of view of "apologetics". From this point of view, it is neither useful nor permissible to appeal to dogmas (e.g. inspiration), since apologetics cannot argue from dogmas of faith. From this angle it would be quite deplorable if we let it appear that a Catholic scholar is not free in the pursuit of his scientific task.

Our paragraph states that the evangelists *always* wrote in such a way as to impart to us "not inventions sprung from the creative faculty of the primitive Christian community, but true and genuine information about Jesus". I suggest that the thought here might be better expressed. Neither faith nor, still less, scholarship can assure us that the evangelists never used a "literary type" which current speech today would describe as "invention"—many instances of this occur in the Old Testament historical books, and there is no *a priori* reason why what happened in the Old Testament should not have happened in the New Testament. So I suggest that before the word "inventions" we should insert the word "mere", and before the word "creative" should be placed the word "simply". I also propose that before the words "about Jesus" should be inserted: "according to their chosen literary type".

In general, in the course of this almost miraculous Council, we have done much to drive out that spirit of fear and excessive anxiety by which at times our labours were hindered. Today I say: Let us not be afraid of scholarly and historical truth. Let us not be afraid that one truth may tell against another truth. Let us not be afraid that our scholars may be lacking in loyalty to the Church and to traditional doctrine. One of two things is true: *either* there is a world-wide conspiracy of scholars to undermine the bases of Christian faith (and a man who can believe that can believe anything); *or* the aim of our scholars is to reach the full, objective and real truth of the Gospel tradition. In this task they play a dual role: they are loyal Catholics; and they are at the same time scientific scholars whose first presupposition is honesty of investigation. Doubtless some will turn liberty into licence—but we must risk this for the sake of a greater good. Doubtless mistakes are made and will be made in this field—but it is one where trial and error are the road to truth. What we want is not the childish comfort which comes of averting our gaze from the truth, but a truly critical scholarship which will enable us to enter into "dialogue" with non-Catholic scholars.

## 5. THE SEPARATED BRETHREN OF THE WEST

*The Relatio on the 2nd Part of Chapter 3 of "De Oecumenismo", presented by the Most Reverend John Carmel Heenan, Archbishop of Westminster, Vice-President of the Secretariat for Promoting Christian Unity, 7th October 1964*

HAVING CONSIDERED the Separated Brethren of the Eastern Churches we now think of those in the West. The title of this Chapter has been changed at the request of many Fathers of the Council. The separated Christians in the West are not just groups of individual Christians but communities each with its own tradition and character as a Church. But some groups of Christians resolutely refuse to call themselves Churches. That is why in the new title we use the expression "Churches and Ecclesiastical Communities". We have done this in order to include all who can properly be called Christians. But we had no intention of touching the question of what is necessary for a Christian Community to fulfil the theological definition of a Church.

The Secretariat for Promoting Christian Unity had the difficult task of finding an expression which would cover all Christian bodies which have resulted from a divided Christendom. In the end we found that all-embracing term "ecclesiastical communities". The communities and Churches with which we are concerned were described in the earlier version as "those which began in the sixteenth century". We now describe them simply as "Separated Brethren in the West". Historically this is more accurate.

As a result of the many suggestions made by the Fathers between sessions we have adopted a new method of presenting our schema. It was not for us, we felt, to attempt a description of other religious bodies. We have been content, therefore, to draw attention to the beliefs and customs they share with Catholics. The first is the recognition of Christ as the one Mediator between God and man. The second is veneration for the Sacred Scriptures. The third is the sacrament of Baptism, while the fourth is the following of Christ in daily life. By showing what Christians have in common we provide some foundation for dialogue with our Separated Brethren.

It seemed right, on the other hand, to mention that doctrines also divide our fellow Christians from ourselves. It is an essential part of the dialogue to make this clear. In trying to give a temperate and balanced presentation we hope to have satisfied all the Fathers. Some, when they read our first version, thought its tone smacked of proselytism. Others feared that we might encourage indifferentism. We have tried to meet the objections of both extremes.

The conclusion of this section is to be read as the summing up not only of this one chapter but of the whole schema on ecumenism. We have summarized the general principles from which the whole work of ecumenism must draw its inspiration. We have stressed both loyalty to the Catholic Faith and our need to respond to the Holy Spirit calling all Christians to that unity which is the will of Christ.

The Holy Father, Paul VI, has said more than once that he wants to follow the example of Pope John, of glorious memory, in making this Second Vatican Council truly pastoral and ecumenical. The Secretariat for Promoting Christian Unity believes that the principles laid down in this schema will enable us to meet the Pope's wishes.

Priests and faithful alike look to the Fathers of the Council as their leaders. Those beloved brethren whom we call separated are nevertheless closely united to us in Christian hope and prayer. They are growing more and more anxious to co-operate with us. The world is awaiting the outcome of this debate on ecumenism. Even those without any religion will carefully study what we have to say about Christian Unity. Here is our great opportunity of showing that it is as true today as it was in the early Church that Christians are recognizable as such because they love one another. I hope, Venerable Brethren, that you will show your good pleasure by recording a unanimous vote.

# 6. THE LAYMAN IN THE CHURCH

*Intervention of the Most Reverend John Carmel Heenan, Archbishop of Westminster, in the name of the Hierarchy of England and Wales, in the Debate on the Lay Apostolate, 12th October 1964*

THIS DOCUMENT, Venerable Brothers, is not only opportune but most necessary to the Church of today. The place of laymen in the life of the Church has completely changed. For over a thousand years few men besides priests and monks were literate. The schools and universities, for the most part founded by the Church, had among their students a majority of ecclesiastics. Not many citizens even among the rich and noble thought it worth-while to learn the art of reading and writing. In the English language and, indeed, in the French the same word was used to describe a priest and a man of learning. That one word, of course, was clerk. It was even worse in Italian since the word *"chierico"* meant "learned" while *"idiota"* was used to describe either a fool or a member of the laity.

This may be the historical reason for the treatment of the laity in Church legislation. In Canon Law they scarcely have a place at all. What is a layman? It is not easy to find a definition. A layman is simply a non-cleric—a negative sort of person. But the faithful of our day are often more learned than the priests. A parish priest no longer has to read and write letters for his flock. It is clear, therefore, that when we talk about lay apostles we do not mean people who are ignorant or uncouth.

All this leads me to make certain comments on the schema concerning the lay apostolate. Let it be said, in the first place, that it is absolutely necessary for our lay apostles to have a careful and deep spiritual training. Although proficient or even outstanding in their knowledge of secular subjects, they still need the formation which theology and asceticism can give them. On this account they need special training even more. For the work of the lay apostolate is sacred and delicate, being ultimately concerned with the salvation of souls.

It is for those who would be lay apostles to put themselves humbly in the hands of their priests for training. It is true the training of the priest himself may have been defective. It is generally agreed that the seminary course needs to be expanded and improved. Although this is true, we must not forget that even young priests fresh from the seminary have finished a course of sacred studies and are capable of providing the laity with the spiritual guidance they need. We talk about the priesthood of the laity, but it must not be thought that the priesthood of the clergy has become in some way less important. This schema on the lay apostolate does well to recall the authority of pastors of souls: "When it is a question of activities and organizations which are not strictly spiritual, it is still the duty of the Hierarchy to lay down and interpret with authority the principles of the moral law."

It is well known that the enemies of the Church do all in their power to create divisions between the clergy and the faithful. It would be most unfortunate if the apostolate of the laity were seen as something in opposition to the apostolate of the clergy. We sincerely praise the authors of this document because they set out to draw together the work of the clergy and laity and make their apostolate one.

Very briefly indeed I want to say a word about the title which appears over one of the paragraphs. The title is: "Catholic Action". Now in some parts of the world this word has assumed a certain political connotation. For that reason it would be better in certain countries if the expression were not used. I hope that each regional conference of bishops will be left free to speak of the Apostolate rather than of Catholic Action.

I want, last of all, to comment on the Secretariat for the Lay Apostolate which it is proposed to set up in Rome. This is something which is bound to fail unless the laity are fully consulted. This Secretariat will be unique among the Secretariats of the Holy See. It would be a disaster to model it on any of the Departments already existing in the Roman Curia. Most of the members of the Secretariat must be chosen from the laity. Let me stress that the faithful take it badly if decisions over matters in which they are well versed are taken without any word of advice being asked from them. Before setting up the Secretariat it is important, therefore, to enquire from the laity themselves how they think it should be set up and how it ought to be run.

Many of our Catholic laity know much more than we do about public affairs, journalism, radio, law, education, medicine and the social services. The proper thing for us to do is to learn from them. It is obviously necessary for this Secretariat to have the guidance of competent ecclesiastics. But this does not mean that all the business must be conducted by prelates or that laymen would not be capable of presiding at any of its meetings. Let the laity be "doers of the word and not hearers only". It is better that the laity should now be invited to accept more responsibility in the Church.

The people to choose for this Secretariat are the men and women who in their own countries have taken a lead in the lay apostolate. But invitations should also besent to those who, being members of no Catholic society or confraternity, nevertheless work tirelessly for the good of the whole community. The value of their apostolate is perhaps the greater because their public spirit gives the Catholic Church a good name in the community. The members of the Secretariat must be typical and exemplary Catholics. We do not want to send to Rome only old gentlemen who are loaded down with ecclesiastical honours. We must also choose some of our young men and women who have to earn their daily bread. A Secretariat made up of people like this can really do good work. It would also show our devoted laity that they have the full confidence of the Hierarchy.

## 7. THE ROLE OF THE LAYMAN

*Address of Mr Patrick Keegan, on behalf of the Lay Auditors, to the Fathers of the Second Vatican Council, 13th October 1964*

IN THE name of the lay Auditors, men and women, present in Rome, I thank the Cardinal Moderators for the honour and opportunity of addressing this great Assembly. I would assure you, Venerable Fathers, that we are very conscious of our responsibility at this historic moment to try, however inadequately, to voice the sentiments of the faithful laity throughout the world.

We have welcomed most warmly the Chapter of the document on the Church dealing with the Laity, giving us a new vision of our active participation in the whole mission of the Church. We have welcomed also the Constitution on the Liturgy which has vitalized our share in the public worship of the Church.

We offer the assurance of our loyal co-operation in fulfilling the noble aims of the document on Christian Unity. And now we have been following with the greatest attention your debate on the Lay Apostolate.

This schema marks for us a point of fulfilment in the historical development of the Lay Apostolate. We sincerely hope that it marks also the beginning of a whole new stage of development.

The schema is the natural outcome of the Church's new awareness of herself. It is also the result of the progressive discovery by men and women of their responsibility and role within the whole apostolate of the Church. All those who work in the different fields of the apostolate will welcome the present debate as a powerful recognition of their efforts. The very existence of the document under discussion is proof that the apostolate of the laity is no luxury nor passing fashion. It means that this apostolate is incorporated into the new dynamism of the Church, seeking new ways to implement the message of the Gospel, seeking new means better adapted to the different social, economic and cultural situations of modern man.

No document could have provided a codification of all that is being done in the different fields of the apostolate. Nor would one have wished that it should. This schema leaves the field open for further developments and at the same time points to the common ground in apostolic endeavour. Because circumstances and needs will differ, precise forms and structures cannot be universally imposed.

In the general report on the schema, we heard with great interest of the Commission's intention to link this schema with other Conciliar documents which directly affect the laity: with, for example, the chapter on the laity in "*De Ecclesia*"; with the Decree on Means of Communication. In particular, we anxiously await the debate on the Church in the Modern World. All this will have immense implications for the responsible activity of the laity both in the spiritual and in the temporal orders.

It is clear that an apostolic lay action must be rooted in the actual situation and needs of the world. And, as we all know, these needs, both spiritual and temporal, are very great.

Yet, whilst it is true that all Christians are called through baptism and confirmation to the apostolate, we must face the fact that few answer that call.

How are the vast majority of Catholics to be made aware of their apostolic responsibility to bear witness in their daily life, as members of a family, as members of the community of the Church and of the whole community? This is the challenge for all those who bear responsibility for Christian formation—for parents, teachers, priests, and for leaders of Catholic groups and organizations. It is here that we see the first role of our organizations. It is clear that association provides the most favourable conditions for Christian formation and for sustaining the individual in the development of his creative potential and in the witness he must bear to the world. The establishment and development of organized groupings should therefore be strongly encouraged.

To help us to fulfil our role, Venerable Fathers, may we presume to appeal through you for priests to give us their indispensable help? It is the priest who brings Christ to us through the sacraments and the Gospels. It is the priest who equips us spiritually to "consecrate the world". Those of us especially who work in lay movements know how much we owe to our brotherly co-operation with our chaplains.

The Lay Apostolate cannot be an isolated entity in the Church. It reaches its fullness in close collaboration with all the other members of the Church. By its very nature it demands a constant and regular exchange between the Hierarchy and the laity. It is for us as lay people to bring to our pastors our experience of the needs of the world in which we live, and to seek from them guidance in our endeavour to respond to these

H

needs. In simple terms, there must be the "family dialogue" of which our Holy Father, Pope Paul, has spoken so frequently and emphasized in his recent Letter *Ecclesiam Suam*.

His Eminence Cardinal Cento, to whom our thanks as to all members of his Commission are due, told us in his introduction to this debate that there is, by wish of her divine Founder, a distinction within the Church between the Hierarchy and the Laity. But this distinction implies no distance. This debate in the Council has done much to bind us together inseparably in the single mission of the Church.

# 8. SCHEMA XIII

*Intervention by the Most Reverend John Carmel Heenan, Archbishop of Westminster, in the Debate on "The Church in the World Today", 22nd October 1964*

IT WOULD be most ungracious if we were not to praise the efforts of the Commission which has produced the document we are now considering. There can be no doubt that the Council Fathers concerned and their advisers have worked hard and have done their best. It is nevertheless quite obvious that the document they have presented to us is unworthy of a General Council of the Church.

If we are to speak at all about the Church in the world of today we must do so in clear unmistakable and down-to-earth terms. For some years not only the faithful but non-Catholics and even unbelievers have been awaiting from this Council wise advice on many grave problems. The Holy See itself has suggested that the Second Vatican Council will make some attempt to solve the complex social problems of our day. The document now before us will therefore be studied with eager hope.

What sort of judgment, Venerable Brothers, do you think the world will pass on this treatise? On some questions, as we know, it is better to say too little than too much. On the subject of world problems, however, it would have been much better to say nothing than produce a set of platitudes. I would like you to call to mind the number of sittings we had when the question of the sources of revelation was so fiercely debated. The theologians, of course, rightly regarded this as a highly important topic. But to the citizens of the wide world, whether Catholic or non-Catholic, a debate of this kind seems like wasting time and beating the air. Having spent such a long time on theological niceties this Council will become a laughing-stock in the eyes of the world if it now rushes breathlessly through a debate on world hunger, nuclear war and family life. People will ask ironically and with good reason what do we really mean when we call this a pastoral Council?

I must speak plainly. This document is going to dash the hopes of everyone who has been awaiting it. Its authors do not seem to realize even to whom the message should be directed. Here is an example of their way of writing: "Christians", they say, "are ready to engage in a dialogue with all men of good will." But surely this is a pointless thing to say. Christians should be ready to conduct a dialogue with anyone, whether or not he is a man of good will. The whole treatise reads more like a sermon than a document of a Council.

We have been given the scheme itself together with certain supplements. The fact is that the scheme even read with the supplements remains obscure and misleading; read on its own it is dangerous and could prove harmful. I would like the Fathers of the Council to consider this question very seriously. We have been told to debate the scheme and to pass over the rest without comment. But if we fail to scrutinize both documents with great care the mind of the Council will have to be interpreted to the world by the specialists who helped the Fathers of the Commission to draw up the documents. God forbid that this should happen! I fear specialists when they are left to explain what the bishops meant.

Between sessions of this Council the Church of God has suffered a great deal from the writings and speeches of some of the specialists. They are few in number but their sound has gone forth to the ends of the earth. These few specialists care nothing for the ordinary teaching authority of the bishops—nor, I regret to say, for that of the Pope. It is idle to show them a papal encyclical in which a point of Catholic doctrine is clearly laid down. They will immediately reply that a Pope is not infallible when writing an encyclical. It really does not seem worth-while for the Pope to write any more encyclical letters since they can apparently no longer be quoted in support of the Faith.

We must protect the authority of the Teaching Church. It is of no avail to talk about a College of Bishops if specialists in articles, books and speeches contradict and pour scorn on what a body of bishops teaches. Until now it has not been a doctrine of the Church that the theologians admitted to the Council are infallible. The theories of one or two must not be mistaken for a general agreement among theologians which has, of course, special authority.

Perhaps the Commission responsible for this document had no chance of success from the outset. They were, in fact, denied the help of experts who really knew their subjects. When you are dealing with the problems of social life you need to consult those who know and live in the world. Now let me ask how many parish priests, how many of the faithful, how many husbands and wives, how many doctors, economists, scientists (especially experts in bio-chemistry and nuclear physics) were at work on this Commission? It is useless in these matters to seek advice only from those who since their youth have spent their lives in monasteries, seminaries or universities. These eminent men may hardly know the world as it really is. The world can be unpleasant and cruel. These scholars often have a childlike trust in the opinions of men in the world. Certainly they are simple as doves but they are not always wise as serpents.

If you are looking for examples of all this you need only study the section on matrimony. Everyone knows that doctors all over the world are busily trying to produce a satisfactory contraceptive pill. This special kind of pill is to be a panacea to solve all sexual problems between husbands and wives. Neither the treatise itself nor the supplements hesitate to prophesy that such a pill is just round the corner. Meanwhile, it is said, married couples and they alone must decide what is right and wrong. Everyone must be his own judge. But, the document adds, the couple must act according to the teaching of the Church. But this is precisely what married people want to be told—what *is* now the teaching of the Church? To this question our document gives no reply. For that very reason it could provide an argument from our silence to theologians after the Council who wish to attack sound doctrine.

The document thus blandly addresses husbands and wives: "Some practical solutions have made their appearance and there are more to come". This is no way for a document of the Church to be composed. When our children ask us for bread, we should not give them a stone.

I strongly appeal for this document to be given to a

new Commission. The treatise itself says that learned men and married couples must work out with theologians ways of understanding more thoroughly the mysteries of nature. But this should be done before and not after a conciliar document is drawn up.

I therefore propose that without delay a new Commission be set up composed of specialists from the laity and priests with long pastoral experience. Then after three or four years let the fourth and final session of the Council be convened to discuss all these social problems. It is true that some of us in this Episcopal College will have gone to our reward. But perhaps we shall then be able to help the Council more by our prayers than we do now by our speeches. One thing is quite certain. It would be a scandal to rush this debate now that we have at last come to really pastoral problems.

## 9. THE SOCIAL ORDER

*Intervention by the Right Reverend Gordon Wheeler, Coadjutor Bishop of Middlesbrough, on Chapter IV of the Schema on "The Church in the World Today", 5th November 1964\**

IN THE interesting section 23 of this schema, dealing with *De Vita Oeconomica et Sociali*, much emphasis is laid upon the need for the equitable distribution of the goods of this earth amongst the peoples of the human family. On page 27, paragraph 5, it is said that the economic and social differences in the modern world constitute an offence against social justice and the essential unity of the human race. But having urged that no effort be spared to lessen and in time to eliminate those differ-

* This intervention was submitted to the Commission after its delivery had been ruled out by the Closure Motion.

ences, the argument is qualified and, in my opinion, weakened by the reminder that personal rights and national characteristics must be respected.

Whilst clearly upholding the right to personal property, I fear lest this assertion, seen in this context, may be used to salve the consciences of those owners of vast properties in certain parts of the world outside whose estates so many of the poor languish. It is easy to understand the appeal of Communism for those who suffer in this way. And it is therefore important that we proclaim unambiguously, both in theory and practice, the Church's clear teaching in this respect.

The goods of this world were destined by God for the benefit of the whole human race and not for any individual, or group or nation. The distribution of the fruits of the earth and the control of productive factors must accord with justice, so that each is given his due and none may usurp for his private enjoyment products and property which should be shared by many.

The Christian defence of private property is only valid in the context of Christian justice augmented by love and compassion. Ownership of property has meaning only in a social context. It must be seen in the light of the legitimate needs of the community. So that a man may be guaranteed his freedom, social security and the means of personal development, he may exercise personal rights of ownership. But these rights carry with them the duty to use his property not merely for his own benefit but also in such a way as not to restrict or damage the rights of others. *Caritas Christi urget nos.*

Large accumulations of personal property may in justice and for the common good be redistributed; and I do not mean unjust confiscation. This task lies ultimately with the civil authorities who must decide upon the best economic solution. Other forms of wealth besides land can be redistributed. Similarly those nations which have a disproportionate share of the world's wealth should in justice correct this imbalance by contributing to the economic needs of other countries. Reference is made to this in paragraph 3 on page 28, but it might usefully be emphasized that such assistance should be altruistic and never undertaken merely for commercial or political gain. Industrialized nations must accept the fact that the development of new industries in the developing countries will bring a demand for free access to their markets.

Finally an appeal is made by the Council on page 30, paragraph 8, to all the faithful to undertake, with all their energy, work that will lead to an increase in the spirit of brotherhood and mutual help between the nations of the world. We owe gratitude to those who voluntarily give their personal service and we should be helping more to do this, financially and otherwise. For many the possibility of any direct part in this work is out of the question. Let them be urged to fulfil their duty by their support of international relief and development organizations whose tremendous task would be rendered much more effective if they were given the financial and moral backing of countless individuals unable personally to take any direct part in this all important work.

In the Epistle of St James we read: "What profits it, my brothers, if anyone says that he has the Faith but does not show it forth by his works" and "Faith, if it has no works, is dead in itself".

The *essence* of communications with the world of our time—and its ultimate acceptance of the Faith—will be achieved above all by the practice of justice and charity.

## 10. THE CHURCH'S ROLE IN THE FIGHT AGAINST WORLD POVERTY

*Intervention by the Very Reverend Gerald Mahon, M.A., Superior General, St Joseph's Society for Foreign Missions, Mill Hill, on Chapter IV of the Schema on "The Church in the World Today", 9th November 1964*

THE PROBLEMS of hunger, world poverty and the so-called population explosion deserve more extended treatment than they are given in the present section of the Schema which, though carefully thought out, is rather compressed. This is, after all, the central problem of our age: that the world is divided into the "haves" who virtually want for nothing, and the "have-nots" who lack almost everything. About this problem the Church must speak out boldly and take energetic action. Otherwise her claim to have dialogue with the world will not be taken seriously.

The First Vatican Council was convened at the height of the industrial revolution. Two years earlier Karl Marx had written *Das Kapital*. Yet the Council did not issue any guidance on social justice within the industrialized nations. There was no word of encouragement from the Church in Council for the proletariat, the victimized working class. They could hardly be expected to lift up their eyes from their misery to rejoice in the definition of infallibility.

In this Second Vatican Council for two and a half years we have discussed with great seriousness matters affecting the internal life of the Church. But now the Council has begun to speak on matters the world is interested in and we have heard from the Council floor a clear call for international social justice that was very much needed. Today the inequalities between *nations* in the world community are as glaring as formerly they were between *classes* within nations. Today it is not the proletariat classes but the proletariat nations that await the outcome of this Council. The poor of the world are looking with anxious eyes to Rome to see if the Church of Christ, lover of the poor, champions their cause. They are waiting for a call for social justice between nations, a call to concrete, effective, sustained action against grinding poverty. Otherwise, they, the hungry of the world, might well say: "We asked for bread, and you gave us a Schema"—and not even a Schema, but a few paragraphs.

As a missionary I know that missionaries are intensely concerned. They work in the midst of this Third World—*le tiers monde*—where, as Cardinal Landazuri of Lima has warned us, 35 million people die every year from hunger or its effects; where 400 million people are hungry; where one and a half thousand million people suffer from the diseases that follow malnutrition.

These facts must arouse the concern of us all.

Some people are inclined to think of social and socio-economic activity as a second-class missionary occupation. They regard it as a sideline, not really part of the Church's mission of salvation. But, Venerable Fathers, this is not what Our Lord taught in the parable of the Good Samaritan where he expressly corrects this over-clerical mentality. The missionary's duty is to preach the full Gospel of Jesus Christ, not only the spiritual part of it. The spiritual, indeed, is all-important and will normally form the major part of missionary work—*sed haec oportet facere et illa non omittere* (We must do the one without omitting the other).

In our complex twentieth-century civilization, with its rapidly expanding population of economically backward peoples, the simple services of the Good Samaritan must be translated into the modern terms of socio-economic assistance on a world scale, always, however, motivated by Christian love.

I therefore propose:

1. In the revised Schema, the abolition of world hunger and world poverty should be given prominence as one of the main themes, in keeping with the importance and urgency of the subject.

2. The Schema should stress the necessity of educating all Christians in their grave responsibility, for the under-privileged of the world, basing its teaching on the demands of international social justice. A vast potential of generosity as yet untapped could be utilized by making still more widely known the admonitions of recent Popes on this topic. In this sphere knowledge begets generosity. In fact, if a clarion call comes from this Council to wage an all-out war on want, even those Catholic agencies which are outstanding in the amount of money they collect would receive a new impetus that would increase their funds and enable them to do more. At present, as administrators of these funds know to their bitter disappointment, even the very generous sums that are available are quite insufficient to grant the requests of the Bishops from developing countries who come to beg, but who often beg in vain, not for themselves but for their under-privileged people.

3. The Council should work for the mobilization of a "Third World" of Christianity, by ecumenical action, against the "third world" of poverty. A special Secretariat, as has been suggested by His Eminence Cardinal Frings and Mr James Norris, should be set up to direct, at the highest level, the Church's war on want. Such a Secretariat should have as its head an outstanding man who would personify the Church's concern for the world's poor. Among the many duties of this Secretariat may I as a missionary be allowed to single out one: to stimulate and co-ordinate missionary partici-

pation in socio-economic action in the developing countries. Its other functions will be dealt with in a written memorandum.

Some striking action on the part of the Council is needed to convince the nations, after the lengthy treatment given to ecclesiastical subjects, that the Church is as concerned about the harsh realities of the world as she is about her own problems. The implementation of these proposals would highlight the fact that the Church is in fact deeply involved in man's struggle to live in this world since her mission is to save human beings, not disembodied souls.

## 11. MORALITY AND WAR

*Intervention by the Most Reverend George Andrew Beck, Archbishop of Liverpool, in the Debate on Chapter IV of the Schema on "The Church in the World Today", 10th November 1964*

I SPEAK in the name of a number of Bishops from England and Wales. About paragraph 25 of the schema entitled "*De Pace Firmanda*", I wish to make three short points.

1. In the first place, we agree that the text of the schema is generally satisfactory, being both balanced and objective. We agree, however, as has been said for other points, that the presentation of the Council statement is set out better in the appendix than in the text which we are discussing.

Great clarity and exactness are needed in paragraph 2, p. 31, especially lines 4–10, in connection with the use of nuclear weapons from which the present problem of peace and war derives its gravity and urgency, since, in the words of Pope John XXIII, "people live in constant fear lest the storm that every moment threatens should break upon them with dreadful violence". The Council must, of course, maintain the traditional doctrine that indiscriminate destruction in which the direct killing of the innocent is sought and achieved must be condemned as murder and as something intrinsically evil. There is place in the schema for some reference to the teaching of Pope Pius XII with regard to biological and chemical warfare which do not receive mention in the text.

The draft statement does in fact repeat the condemnation of Pope Pius XII and of Pope John XXIII (*Pacem in Terris, A.A.S.*, 1963, pp. 286–7) of any weapon whose effect cannot be estimated and controlled. I would suggest, however, that it is important to make clear that this is not a universal condemnation of the use of nuclear weapons. There may well exist objects which in a just war of defence are legitimate targets of nuclear weapons even of vast force. To attack a ballistic missile or a satellite missile in the outer atmosphere would, for example, be a legitimate act of defence, and with just proportion duly preserved, it might require the use of a weapon of vast power. If, as I think is correct, legitimate targets for nuclear weapons may in fact exist, the Council should not condemn the possession and use or these weapons as essentially and necessarily evil.

2. In the second place, we must remember that responsibility for the use of nuclear weapons and for all decisions concerning peace and war rests with those who exercise supreme authority in the State. The Council has a duty to express sympathy and consideration for those who carry the heavy burden of this responsibility. The government of a country has the duty to protect not only the lives and the property of its

citizens but even more the spiritual and cultural values,
which are the inheritance of a people or a nation. The
government of a country has a grave duty to do everything in its power to promote justice and prevent war.
It must do this by peaceful means to the limit of its
power, but it may be true that in certain circumstances
peace can be assured only by what has been called "the
balance of terror" by the threat of the use of nuclear
weapons as a deterrent against unjust aggression. Let us
not too readily condemn these governments which
succeed and which have succeeded in keeping peace,
however tentative, in the world by the use of such
means. Millions of people owe them gratitude. Let the
Council make clear, therefore, that it does not demand
of governments that they decide on a unilateral aban-
donment of nuclear weapons merely because of the
very real and possibly proximate danger that these
weapons may be used in an unjust and immoral way.
To turn the other cheek is a counsel of perfection addressed to individuals, not to governments, who have a
grave duty to defend the citizens entrusted to their
authority.

3. In the third place, I hope that the text of the
schema, in lines 25–35, will be strengthened. The first
duty and one of the utmost gravity for all governments
is to work in an active and practical way for the establishment of an international order in which war is out-
lawed as an instrument of policy. The Council must
repeat the teaching of Pope Pius XII and Pope John
XXIII about the duty of all governments to work towards organic, progressive and mutually agreed disarmament, so that in Pope John XXIII's words weapons may be reduced on both sides, simultaneously.
The Council must emphasize that equal security must
be given to all peoples (Pope Pius XII, Christmas
Message 1955). Above all, it must emphasize the duty

which all men must accept of striving to establish the order of justice among nations, and of setting up juridical and administrative machinery for the peaceful solution of international differences.

## 12. CATHOLIC SCHOOLS

*Intervention by the Most Reverend George Andrew Beck, Archbishop of Liverpool, in the Debate on Christian Education, 18th November 1964*

THIS DOCUMENT, as the Relator has said, does not correspond with the original aims of the Commission. From a discussion concerning Catholic schools, it has now become a short, uneven and more general statement on Christian education. We think this a pity.

I should like to make three points.

1. The rights of parents to educate their children according to their conscience should be given a much more prominent part in the statement. No mention of these rights appears in the document until paragraph 4. They are, however, so fundamental that their proper place should be at the beginning of the statement. Emphasis on the rights of parents, apart from the fact that they are rooted in natural justice, is important for two practical reasons.

(*a*) In the present age the Church should show herself as the defender of the rights of all parents, and not only of Catholics. Neither the Church nor Catholic parents wish to claim a monopoly of special treatment from civil governments. Every parent has the right to bring up his children in his religious belief and according to his conscience. As Pope John XXIII so aptly put it, "Parents have the strongest possible right (*potissi-*

*mum ius*) to bring up and educate their children."
Hence, if circumstances make it practically possible
parents should be helped to fulfil this duty by the public
authority. I suggest that the statement should include
paragraph 6 of the former draft "Concerning Catholic
Schools". It reads as follows: "the rights of parents,
distributive justice and the common good of society
require that public funds and other forms of assistance
destined for schools should be available for all schools
which are not harmful to the common good without
distinction or discrimination."

(*b*) Catholic parents are citizens. They pay rates and
taxes like their fellow citizens. Their rights should be
recognized by the public authorities. And in fact in
many parts of the world they are recognized at least to
some extent so that Catholic parents are able with a
quiet conscience to send their children to Catholic
schools without an unfair or too heavy financial burden
being imposed on them.

2. In paragraph 7 mention is made that the Church
is "conscious of its own right freely to build and conduct
schools". But the basis of this claim is not explained. No
mention is made of the Church's divine commission to
teach: "Go therefore and teach ye all nations". As far
as I understand the statement, no juridical claims are
made on behalf of the Church as a perfect society in
relation to civil governments. This omission may well be
deliberate policy on the part of the authors of the statement. Such a claim would seem difficult to justify,
particularly with those who do not accept the authority
of Christ or the truth of His revelation. This seems to
me, however, to be a defect in a conciliar document
which deals with Christian education.

3. The statement rightly insists on page 13 that the
provision of Catholic schools is a service which the
Church renders to society. If Catholic schools were not

established, the civil authorities would be obliged to provide other schools from their own resources. And further, the education, religious and moral, given in Catholic schools should exercise a good influence on the whole of society. The products of these schools are trained to be good citizens as well as good Catholics. Here is a further argument for assistance, at least in part from public funds. It is not, indeed, an argument based on justice but on the recognition of the service which such schools give to the State. When civil governments give support to denominational schools they show themselves to be in practice defenders of the principle of toleration and religious freedom.

It is quite certain that in a world of expanding education there must be many more Catholic schools. They can be a precious instrument in promoting that *aggiornamento* which is the main purpose of this Council. They can offer help to governments in every country. We should therefore express our gratitude to those governments which recognize the value of Christian education today and offer financial assistance to Catholic schools. In my own country, as in Scotland, Ireland, Holland, and other parts of the world, the government recognizes the rights of parents, at least in part, and the value of Catholic schools. In this assembly I willingly express our gratitude for the help they give not only for schools but especially in assisting us to establish and maintain Catholic teacher training colleges. For, in fact, as the statement says so well in its last paragraph, we owe a very great debt of gratitude to our teachers, both men and women, under whose generous and devoted care Christian education is turned from a beautiful theory into an activity of real and lasting value. It is on the teachers that the efficacy of Christian education ultimately depends.

I

# 13. MIXED MARRIAGES

*Intervention by the Most Reverend John Carmel Heenan, Archbishop of Westminster, in the name of the Hierarchy of England and Wales, in the Debate on the Sacrament of Matrimony, 20th November 1964*

I AM speaking in the name of the whole Hierarchy of England and Wales and of bishops from many other countries.

We can say of this schema what has often been said in recent days in this hall about other schemata—it is good, indeed, excellent. Though it reflects great credit on the Commission which prepared it—especially on the *periti*—it is nevertheless much too brief.

Holy Matrimony is a sacrament of the greatest dignity. It is in a way at the centre of the whole social life of Christians. St Paul said to the Ephesians: "This is a great sacrament and I speak in Christ and in the Church" (Ephesians 5.32). A noble and really beautiful schema must be composed before the next session. It should deal fully with the theological, biblical and, above all, the pastoral aspects of marriage. Some of the things found in the famous Schema 13 would be more suitably put into this schema. But perhaps I said enough about Schema 13 the other day!

I am delighted at the proposals for a more adequate preparation for marriage and the speeding up of the work of Marriage Tribunals. Some words of the schema I would like to see written in letters of gold: "Pastors should treat the non-Catholic gently and with respect when a couple comes to arrange a mixed marriage. He must in due season warn the couple of the very real difficulties which arise in a mixed marriage not only for the parties themselves but also for their children."

I say that these words should be written in letters of gold
for two reasons. First, because for a young couple inten-
ding to marry, this first meeting with the parish priest is
of the utmost importance. If, as our schema urges, the
priest is kind, understanding and full of charity, the
Church will appear to the couple to be a real mother.
The good will of the non-Catholic meeting a priest perhaps for the first time can easily be won or lost at this
first interview. My second reason is that the schema does
not hesitate to stress that by their very nature mixed
marriages produce many grave problems. These problems and difficulties are not less real because we are
living in ecumenical days. In fact you might say that in
some way the difficulties have become greater. Because of the way in which some ecumenists speak the
simple faithful easily credit that there is no longer any
real distinction of Jew or Greek, Catholic or Protestant.
But once a marriage has been contracted husbands and
wives soon learn that there are still abundant differences.
It is obviously good, as the schema so wisely says, to
warn young people against choosing a partner by a
kind of blind instinct.

I am wholeheartedly in agreement with what is proposed for the future celebration of mixed marriages.
Until now in many places the ceremonies for a mixed
marriage were so stripped of solemnity and joy that they
were more suitable for a funeral than a wedding.
There was no blessing of the ring, no candles or flowers
and—what used to make the bride burst into tears—
there was no organ! It is perfectly clear that if the
Church grants a dispensation she should do so gra-
ciously, magnanimously and in an open-handed way.
The wedding day should be both beautiful and happy
even though the marriage is a mixed marriage. Let the
Church show herself as a real mother not only to the
Catholic but to the non-Catholic as well.

Everybody knows that the chief difficulty about a mixed marriage concerns the religious upbringing of the children. The difficulty does not always arise out of the burning faith and piety of husband and wife. As often as not family traditions and prejudice on one side or another are the cause of the trouble.

Before we examine the proposals in this schema we must look at the problems of mixed marriages in a realistic way. In our country at least, by far the majority of mixed marriages take place between Catholics and those who are Protestants only in name. Usually the non-Catholic partner is not a church-goer of any kind. For twenty years I worked in parishes in the East End of London and I therefore speak with some experience. Only rarely did I find the non-Catholic partner of a mixed marriage to be a really active member of any religious community. For this reason the promises to bring up the children as Catholics rarely caused difficulty. That is why I think it would be better to leave the promises by the partners as the normal rule of law. When a mixed marriage takes place between a Catholic and what we may call for want of a better word a practising Protestant, special rules could be drawn up in a new schema.

In cases of this kind the problem is very real. But for the rest there is very little difficulty in securing the agreement of a non-Catholic to the Catholic upbringing of the children. The probable reason is the religious indifference so widespread in our part of the world. What I have said of England is also true, I imagine, of Australia, New Zealand, U.S.A. and at least the English-speaking parts of Canada.

Experience has shown us that even Protestants who go to church are more often than not—I do not say always—ready to agree to the Catholic education of their children. We must not forget that it need be in no way against the conscience of a non-Catholic to agree to the children being brought up as Catholics. Other Christian Churches do not claim to be the one true Church. That, however, is the claim that Catholics make for their Church. Naturally I do not know if in the fourth session someone is going to suggest that such a claim should be condemned as being dangerous triumphalism!

If the non-Catholic cannot with a good conscience promise that the children will be brought up as Catholics there should be no attempt at coercion. It is sufficient for the non-Catholic not to object to the promise being made by the Catholic party. But in saying this the text of the schema is not at all clear. I assume that it means to say that the non-Catholic without giving promises will agree to abide by the promises made by the Catholic to bring up the children in the Faith. But as the text is now worded it could mean that the non-Catholic might agree to the promise being made without any intention of allowing it to be kept. So the text is in need here of clarification.

I would also like to propose that the expression "so far as I can" should be omitted on page 13. According to the schema the Catholic is required to make a sincere and conscious promise that all children born of the marriage will be baptized and brought up in the Catholic Faith. Those are the terms of the promise. I cannot see, therefore, why there is any need to add "so far as I can". Obviously no one is bound to attempt the impossible. But the words could have a rather different implication. They might mean that the Catholic is not bound by the promises if they become hard to fulfil. In that case the words should be struck from the text. Otherwise it would be as if the Church were saying: "It is not necessary to put up any fight for your children. For the sake of peace by all means let them abandon the

Faith." This would indeed be a new and astonishing doctrine for the Church to preach. Venerable Brothers, the Vatican Council was called by good Pope John to renew not to destroy the Catholic Church.

I would like to say, last of all, that if our text is to be truly ecumenical it ought to say something about the way a mixed marriage is to be celebrated when the non-Catholic party is an active member of another religious community. It is my view—and here I am speaking for myself alone—that there is no reason why, after the marriage has taken place in the Catholic church, the bride and bridegroom should not if they wish go along to the church of the non-Catholic partner to pray and receive a blessing.

# IV. PRESS CONFERENCES

*Each Thursday afternoon throughout the session a Press Conference was given under the auspices of the Information Office of the Hierarchy of England and Wales. The following are summaries of some of the addresses given by speakers at these Conferences.*

# 1. PROSPECTS FOR THE
## THIRD SESSION

*Conference given by Most Reverend John Carmel Heenan,
Archbishop of Westminster, 18th September 1964*

LET ME make it clear in discussing prospects for the
third session, that I have no inside information. It is
impossible to predict with certainty what is going to
happen in this Council, but perhaps we shall be able
to make some thoughtful guesses.

I have tried to diagnose the atmosphere of this first
week. It is certainly different from that of the other two
sessions. There is a sense of urgency and quite obviously
this is shared by those who are responsible for the direction of the Council. One small indication of this is that
the venerable Cardinal Bea was cut off before he had
finished his first speech. It is always a sign that the
Moderators mean business when they refuse to allow
even Cardinals to exceed the ten minutes limit.

There is evidence of a much more professional attitude on the part of the bishops. They know why they
are here and what they have to do. All sense of novelty
has gone and they recognize each other as collabora-
tors in a serious operation. Whether or not collegiality
will be officially recognized by the Council, the friendship between the bishops of so many nations is both real
and important. Whenever and wherever the bishops
have met this week, they have immediately begun to
discuss the work of the Council. Whereas in other sessions it has taken a few weeks for the bishops to organize
themselves, during this first week meetings between
groups of bishops have already taken place in national
colleges and wherever rooms could be found. The

bishops are studying, discussing and praying harder than ever.

Nobody within the Council now talks about conservatives and progressives. These were always rather inappropriate labels, but now they look merely foolish. The bishops of the third session are pastors of souls anxious above all to find ways of making the Church a more efficient instrument in the hands of God and of making her better understood throughout the world. The bishops are realizing more and more that this Council is above all intended to be a pastoral Council.

I think that the key to success in the third session will be the realization that this is Pope John's Council. Pope Paul has repeatedly made it clear that he shares Pope John's views. We can be sure, therefore, that the Pope wants this third session to be run as Pope John would have wished. Again and again Pope John said that this Council was not called to define new dogmas or to settle theological disputes. It was significant that Cardinal Tisserant reminded us of this before the first day's debate.

Pope John showed his determination to keep the Council truly pastoral during the first session. When the battle was joined about the nature of Revelation and the Council was divided almost bitterly between rival camps, Pope John did not hesitate to intervene. He felt that most of the bishops had previously known little of the controversy about the Sources of Revelation. He, therefore, knew that they had not come to Rome on fire to take part in disputes of this kind. With typical simplicity and shrewdness Pope John withdrew the debate from the floor of St Peter's and made about forty of us debate the question behind closed doors. It is remarkable how quickly prima donnas cease to be temperamental when in private.

One indication of the determination of the bishops

not to waste time is that the only speech received with applause was that of a bishop, who said that his points had been made by somebody else so that he would not have any more to say. Similarly the debate on the Blessed Virgin Mary has not been allowed to develop into a firework display. The only question which may cause division amongst the Fathers of the Council is the expression "mediatrix of all graces". Certainly nobody wants to play down the place of Our Lady in the Catholic way of life. But there are many good arguments for avoiding this phrase in a Conciliar document.

We come back to where we started. Pope John wanted nothing said in this Council which could be interpreted as introducing new doctrine. The whole question of Mary as the mediatrix of all graces raises issues which this Council was not summoned to solve.

Everyone would like to know if this is to be the final session. Any bishop who has a pastor's heart must want these Roman journeys to end, so that he can be back with his flock.

But the whole Church of God is more important than any diocese. The question is, whether or not the work of the Council can be finished within ten weeks. It would be a completely unsatisfactory solution to agree on a few general principles and leave experts to decide how to interpret the wishes of the Fathers of the Council. Many of the bishops may well feel that the *periti* who would be charged with this work might not all hold views which the bishops share. The mind of the Fathers must therefore be made clear before Post-Conciliar Commissions begin their work. If this can be achieved by the end of November, at least so far as the main business of the Council is concerned, my hope is that the Conciliar Commissions will go on quietly with their work for two or three years and that the final word will be said in a fourth session.

## 2. THE COLLEGIALITY ISSUE

*Conference given by the Right Reverend Thomas Holland, Bishop of Salford, 24th September 1964*

No COUNCIL will say the last word about the Church. This word "Collegiality" leaves much unexplained. But it is a definite advance. The effort has been well worth-while; the votes of the last few days would alone justify a Council. They may be regarded as the heart of Vatican II: they fulfil the main expectations.

Vatican I opened up one corner of the mystery and was interrupted: even the vision of the primacy was incomplete.

It is to be remembered that these great efforts of the Church to know herself and give a clear outline to her knowledge are all directed to Christ's will. There has been a search into Scripture and Tradition to find *what HE designed*. There is no question of creating novelties, but of giving fresh utterance to the old design.

Collegiality gives coherent utterance to a number of truths clearly found in the sources.

Christ gave His authority to a group which is structural in the Church: it must go on. Present-day bishops are that group. There is no group without the successor of Peter giving unity and strength to it. Vatican I saw this Head of the group and delineated clearly his powers. But the peak emerged without the range. A single commanding height was the impression. Many misunderstood and thought the peak rose sheer and isolated from the plain.

It was no use pointing to the Church's own documents: e.g. Canon 288, where the supreme authority of the Church is clearly shown in a group—in a General Council. People said there would be no more Councils: that Vatican I made them superfluous.

John XXIII answered that: Vatican II is the answer. And Vatican II has now shown that the powers of the Head—even outside a General Council—are still held in the group. All that was defined about the Head is here clearer, in its full context. No word of Vatican I has been unsaid: the Holy Father's powers as Head of the Church are more firmly and clearly affirmed in the context of the permanent College of Apostles.

The special prominence given to the Pope, the incompleteness of Vatican I, has its providential gains. The eyes of the world were uniquely on the Popes: they have been giants: there was no question of their failing under scrutiny. But they appeared remote, in isolation.

The world unifies itself: vital interpretation of countries and continents goes on apace. Providentially now, in this unifying world, the Pope's unity with the whole Church will be emphasized through collegiality: he will be seen, through the bishops, in vital contact with all parts of the Church.

What new developments may be expected?

In general a new, vigorous integration of the bishops into concern for the whole Church. The details will be decided later—perhaps some very soon.

A senate of bishops? An association of the bishops in the production of encyclicals? A new co-ordination of the regular clergy with the diocesan? (The Regulars depend upon the Pope: through him they come into the general service of the College of which he is head.)

At the level of the bishops among themselves, the new understanding of their corporate concern for the whole Church will work out in a more free association of the national hierarchies for common problems. We shall have to come to the service of dioceses short of personnel resources in more co-ordinated efforts.

Ecumenically, there may be considerable repercussions.

Our own people's reverence for their bishops will have more articulate expression.

## 3. THE JEWS AND RELIGIOUS LIBERTY

*Conference given by the Most Reverend John Carmel Heenan, Archbishop of Westminster, Vice-President of the Secretariat for Promoting Christian Unity, 26th September 1964*

### 1. The Jews

I propose for a moment to ignore current controversies in order to enquire how, in the first place, the Council came to consider the question of the Jews. This came about in the context of Ecumenism. It is impossible to study Catholic theology in isolation from the Old Testament. The new law cannot be interpreted without the old. It was natural, therefore, to extend Christian Ecumenism to include the Jews. It is important to stress that the motives for including the Jews in the schema on Ecumenism were exclusively theological and spiritual.

It was only after the publication of the original schema that the Secretariat for Promoting Christian Unity was made to face controversial issues. Bishops living in predominantly Moslem areas made it plain that there was some danger lest Moslems should become aggrieved that the Jews alone were given consideration at the Vatican Council. Those bishops living in areas where Buddhists or Hindus predominate similarly maintained that the faithful in Asia might suffer unless others besides Jews were mentioned.

The Secretariat has met these objections by introducing a second part to the Declaration dealing with non-Christians who are not Jews. It must be said, however, that the demand for the inclusion of non-Jews may have been based on a misconception. We had no political motive of any kind for introducing the Jews into the schema on Ecumenism. The chief reason why the Jews were singled out is because of their unique relationship with Christianity.

There was another reason why the Secretariat felt it proper to introduce a section on the Jews. In our generation no race has suffered more violent and widespread persecution than the Jews. Millions of Jews during this century have been tortured and put to death for reasons of race or religion. It seemed fitting that the compassion of the great assembly of Council Fathers should be expressed. The opportunity was taken of declaring our abhorrence of this treatment and of condemning anti-semitism and all racial and religious intolerance.

At the last session it was hoped that the whole schema on Ecumenism might have been approved. But it became clear during the debate that many of the Fathers had reservations. Cardinal Bea, therefore, wisely refrained from pressing the matter to a vote. Many of the Fathers in the Middle East and Asia might have voted against the schema for the reasons explained above. But if a considerable number of votes had been cast against the schema "*De Judaeis* the world might have thought that many bishops are, in fact, anti-semitic. This would have been deplorable. It was wise to postpone the voting until mention could be made of other non-Christian religions and so prevent any adverse reaction.

The reformed schema has created a great deal of misunderstanding especially in England and in the United States of America. The headline in the *Jewish Chronicle* for 11th September reads: "REVISED CHAPTER ON JEWS CAUSES DEEP DISMAY". There are two chief

objections. The first is the quotation from St Paul's
Epistle to the Romans (11.25): "I must not fail,
brethren, to make this revelation known to you, or else
you might have too good a conceit of yourselves. Blindness has fallen upon a part of Israel, but only until the
tale of the Gentile nations is complete; then the whole
of Israel will find salvation. . . ." From this it was
assumed that the main motive of including the Jews in
the schema on Ecumenism was to convert them.

This was to misunderstand the whole nature of
Ecumenism. Its object is not the conversion either of
non-Catholics or of non-Christians. Ecumenism sets out
to break down barriers between religious denominations in order that each may come to know and better
understand the other. Ecumenism is an essay not in
polemics but in charity. The dialogue is not a battle
of wits. Its intention is not for one side to score a victory
but for each side to emerge with deeper knowledge of
the other.

It must be admitted, however, that the ultimate end
of all ecumenical activity is the unity of the sons of God.
All Christians—whether of East or West, Protestant
and Catholic—work and pray for reunion in the one
Holy Catholic Church. The unity of all the brethren of
Christ is the hope of every Christian. But Ecumenism
for the Church of Rome is not a plot to destroy the faith
of Protestants, Jews or any other believers.

It is difficult to understand how the motives of the
Secretariat came to have been misinterpreted. There is
no more reason for Jews than for Protestants to accuse
the Secretariat of proselytism. Rabbi Hechel is reported
in the *Jewish Chronicle* as saying that he "would be ready
to go to Auschwitz if faced with the alternative of conversion or death". This is, of course, rhetorical language.
True conversion means the free acceptance of the Faith.
It was far from the mind of the Secretariat to use the

statement *"De Judaeis"* to attack the beliefs of our Jewish brethren.

The second objection to the new draft is that it omits any reference to deicide. In the former schema these words were used: "Although a large part of the chosen people remains separated from Christ it would be unjust . . . to call it a deicide people since the Lord by His passion and death has atoned for the sins of all men, which were the cause of the passion and death of Jesus Christ (Lk. 23.34, Acts 3.17, I Cor. 2.8); the death of Christ was not caused by a whole people then living and much less than by a people of today." The new schema reduces this paragraph to a single sentence: ". . . Equally all should be on their guard not to impute to the Jews of our time that which was perpetrated in the Passion of Christ." I understand why the Jews feel aggrieved. To have removed the reference absolving the Jewish people from deicide at first sight appears equivalent to repeating the accusation. I do not know why the wording was changed. Perhaps the reason will be revealed during the debate in the Council. To me personally the expression "deicide" has always seemed rather odd. That Jesus Christ was condemned to death by the Sanhedrin is a fact of history. In that sense it is correct to say that Jesus Christ was killed by Jews. But this is not to say, or even to suggest, that the Jews, having recognized Christ as God, resolved to kill him. If the Jews had accepted Christ's claim to be God they obviously would not have put Him to death. What really needed to be stated is that the Jewish people *as such* cannot be held guilty for the death of Christ. This was not true of the main body of the Jewish people even at the time when Christ was crucified. It is even more obviously untrue to impute responsibility for the death of Our Lord to the Jews of a later age and of our own time.

K

It is important to say that the question of the culpability of the Jews for the death of Jesus has been given an altogether exaggerated importance. I do not believe that most Christians think of the Jews when thinking of the passion and death of Our Lord. Every Catholic in the world has been taught to recite daily the Act of Contrition. In this prayer these words occur: "I beg pardon for all my sins because they [my sins] have crucified my loving Saviour, Jesus Christ. . . ." It is part of Catholic theology that the Son of God died to redeem mankind from sin. It is of Faith that Christ is the victim of sin and that all sinners—Christians as well as non-Christians—are in this sense responsible for His death.

It is not for me to anticipate the debate in St Peter's on the new draft of "*De Judaeis*". I can only hope that it will be passed with an impressive majority. I am quite certain that there is no anti-Jewish feeling among the Fathers of the Council.

## 2. *Religious Liberty*

At the beginning of the Declaration on religious liberty it is made clear that the work of Ecumenism cannot prosper if any doubt exists that all Christians share a belief in religious liberty. That is why religious liberty is being discussed under the guidance of the Secretariat for Christian Unity. But it is evident that even if there were no talk of Christian Unity, any Council called in the middle of the twentieth century would have to take account of the question of liberty. It may seem strange that never before has religious liberty been the subject of discussion in a General Council. But the fact is that the need for the Church to protect liberty has become really urgent only in recent years.

Liberty has been threatened in our times in a way hitherto unknown to history. There have been absolute monarchs and tyrannical rulers in past centuries. What is new is making a cult of tyranny under the name of ideology. This is one of the reasons why the Church has been forced to turn its attention to the whole question of freedom. The threat to liberty is now epidemic and the time has come for a solemn proclamation from an Ecumenical Council.

The inviolability of a man's conscience is a fundamental requirement for all freedom. It is not new for the Church to make a plea for religious freedom. There have probably been more Christians put to death for their faith in the last fifty years than in any comparable period in history. The Church has tirelessly protested against the suppression of religious freedom in Nazi and Communist States throughout the world. But the Statement does not seem to be primarily concerned with the persecution of religion. Cardinal Koenig, in a most moving speech on Thursday, was severely critical of the Statement because it passes over almost in silence the crucifixion of liberty which is part of the Communist creed.

The Statement is concerned to proclaim the Church's belief in religious freedom for all mankind. It has often been alleged of Catholics that they believe in tolerance only when they themselves are in a minority. It is said that in countries where the overwhelming majority of citizens is Catholic the same view is not upheld. The Statement is obviously more concerned to correct this view than to make a fresh protest against the persecution of the Church by atheistic Communism. In the notes which accompany the Statement the development of the Church's doctrine on liberty is outlined. In his encyclical *Pacem in Terris* Pope John had a great deal to say about the dignity and liberty of the human person. He reminded us that while condemning error we must always cherish the person who errs. This was typical of the kindly attitude of Pope John, but it was by no means a new departure in Catholic theology. The distinction between the sin and the sinner has always been traditional in the Church.

Pope John was following the example of his predecessor, Pope Pius XII, who had not remained silent on the question of religious freedom. Both in audiences and encyclicals he made reference to this subject. Thus in his encyclical *Mystici Corporis*, having spoken of his desire for the return of all to the one fold of Christ, he said: "It is absolutely necessary that this must come about because men freely desire to enter the Church. For no one can believe unless he wishes to do so. Those who do not believe should never be forced to enter the Church, to approach the altar or to receive the sacraments. The faith must be completely free because it is the submission of the mind and the will."

The subject matter of the Statement has been described as delicate and difficult. One of the reasons for this is that the traditions of different countries tend to give people opposite concepts of freedom. Freedom itself is not easy to define. It is not mere tolerance which is passive and negative. Freedom is active and positive. Some countries are regarded as being more devoted to freedom than others. Citizens of the United States, for example, as members of a fairly new nation are inspired by the ideals of liberty written into the United States Constitution. But this Constitution is, in fact, a modern version of ideas deeply rooted not only in Christian, but in Jewish and classical traditions. Above all, these ideas of liberty are embedded in the Common Law of England. Magna Carta is much more than a name to the British people.

Whatever principles be laid down by the Council the actual exercise of freedom ultimately depends upon those who hold authority in the State. It is not difficult to frame laws which give the impression of freedom although, in fact, they may mask intolerance. Let me take the example of Stalin's Constitution for Soviet Russia. Article 124 reads: "Freedom of worship and freedom of anti-religious propaganda are guaranteed to all citizens". This meant, in effect, that citizens could attack religion but—since religious propaganda is illegal—the believer could be punished for preaching the Gospel.

Although without the goodwill of those in authority liberty cannot be enjoyed, it is nevertheless right for the Church to lay down the principles. It is important to remember that the idea of freedom as the right of all men is a fairly modern notion. For centuries civilized States took slavery for granted. Therefore we should not be too surprised that is has been left to a General Council in the twentieth century to consider the subject of liberty.

But it is important that the Council should speak in an unequivocal fashion, because not only Christians but all believers and even non-believers await the Council's pronouncement with deep concern. Pope Paul VI is conscious of the need for a Conciliar Statement and has stressed its importance. He said, according to the *Osservatore Romano* of 18th April 1964, during an audience the previous day—"The Church is preoccupied with the question of religious liberty. It is a question of far-reaching importance and the Council realizes it. We have every right to hope for the promulgation of a text which will have significance not only for the Church but for the countless number of people who will feel affected by an official pronouncement on this question."

Since a Statement of this kind at a General Council is unprecedented, it is not easy to know in what terms the Decree should be made. The Statement could easily have been allowed to grow into a politico-philosophical treatise. Equally it could have become a dogmatic thesis on the nature of truth and the right of man to be intolerant of error. But the Vatican Council is pastoral and therefore has based its decisions on the nature and dignity of human personality. A man has the duty—and therefore the right—of obeying his conscience. But notice that the expression "liberty of conscience", like the expression "liberty of thought", is not strictly speaking accurate. A man can refuse to follow his conscience—just as he can refuse to admit the evidence of his senses—but conscience itself is a dictator: hence the common expression "Dictates of Conscience". Freedom of conscience really means that a man must be left free in choosing to accept or reject what his conscience tells him is right and good.

The Council is setting out to show that all men should be free to practise their religion and that no man should be penalized because of his religious beliefs. This is a principle easy enough to lay down but not always easy to follow in practice. There are some religious sects which normal men regard as fanatical. Their creed may be founded, for example, upon hatred of those who differ from them in religion. It might be the duty of the State to curb the activities of sects of this kind. In this event the adherents of the sect would claim that they were being persecuted—whereas the State is merely doing its duty by protecting other citizens.

It is part of the religious instinct of man to be a crusader. In Christian terms we call this the "missionary spirit". One of the most delicate problems of religious freedom is to know what limits, if any, should be set on missionary activity. This can be put another way by asking—what is the difference between conversion and proselytism? There is no easy formula to use in reply to this question. The difficulty is faced by a

State whose citizens are subjected to missionary activities. Is it possible to say that Catholics everywhere must always have the right to attempt to make converts, if we deny the same right to others who are conscientiously following their beliefs?

Conscience must be a man's guide, but—and here is the most delicate aspect of the problem—his conscience may be in error. For the individual Catholic the problem is not serious because the Church gives infallible guidance in faith and morals. But most of mankind is not within the Catholic Church and is without this infallible guidance. If Catholics are in authority in a State, have they the right or duty to allow non-Catholic missionaries to propagate what the Catholic Church declares to be false doctrine? The schema answers affirmatively, but bishops from Catholic areas where unrest has been stirred up by Protestant missionaries may give no more than a *iuxta modum* to this view.

What should be the attitude of the State to religion? It is fashionable now to talk about the pluralistic society in which there is no one moral code binding all citizens. It is clear that the State has no right to suppress religion—but has it the right to support one religion more than another? Is it against the principles of religious liberty to have an Established Church in different States?

Not all are agreed on what is meant by State neutrality in matters of religion. It need not mean that the State must stand apart from religion. It could mean that the State is willing to give support to the various religions of its citizens. We know, for example, how differently States interpret their duty towards denominational schools. Although in England the Anglican is the Established Church, Catholic schools receive precisely the same generous grants as are given to Anglican schools. In other countries State aid of every kind is withheld from church schools. These I give as examples of the difficulty and delicacy of the Vatican Council in making a detailed Statement on religious freedom. The matter is now under debate and we can only say that it is a welcome sign that the Catholic Church should stand so strongly for religious freedom. The reputation of the Church has often been attacked on the grounds of her intolerance. I hope and believe that this Conciliar document will be passed by an impressive majority so that the world may see where Catholics stand on the question of freedom.

## 4. THE CONSTITUTION ON DIVINE REVELATION

*Conference given by the Right Reverend Christopher Butler, O.S.B., Abbot of Downside, 1st October 1964*

THE CURRENT debate on this draft document recalls the central drama of the first session of the Council. In November 1962 the Council turned from its long discussion of the reform of public worship to debate a document prepared before the opening of the Council and entitled "The Sources of Revelation". This draft fell into two parts: a theological exposition of the complementary roles of Scripture and Tradition in transmitting the content of the Christian faith; and a more particular examination of scriptural issues, with special reference to the historical value of the Gospels. It came under very heavy fire in the debate, especially for its treatment of the theological question. After about four days' discussion, a vote showed that the preponderant view was that the draft was not suitable as a basis for drawing up a Constitution on the important subject-matter involved. Although this view failed to secure the two-thirds majority required by the regulations, John XXIII took the only sensible line: he personally withdrew the document, and set up a mixed commission from among the members of the Doctrinal Commission and the Secretariat for Unity, to prepare a new draft. The present draft is a further revision of this new draft, made in the light of written animadversions on it since it was first circulated last year.

The draft thus revised retains the general structure of the original, unhappy document. It is significant that its title is new. It is a Constitution, not on the Sources of Revelation, but on Divine Revelation. In fact, the governing aim of its authors has been to avoid appearing to commit the Council to either of two views about Scripture and Tradition which are in living controversy with each other in the contemporary Church. According to one of these views, Scripture is an incomplete source for the discovery of the original and permanently valid contents of the Christian revelation. The other view holds that there is a sense in which Scripture contains, at least implicitly, the whole contents of the Catholic faith; on this view, Tradition's role is not so much to supplement as to draw out and interpret what is contained in Scripture.

At the time of the Reformation, the Protestants sought to justify their radical attitude to the Catholic *status quo* by arguing that the true nature of Christianity must be determined by appeal to Scripture alone. The reply of the Council of Trent was that the "deposit of faith" was preserved by Scripture *and* Tradition; and that the appeal to the evidence of Tradition was not only lawful, but necessary. As the antagonists of this great debate hardened in their positions it became usual for Catholic controversialists and teachers to interpret Trent as meaning that there were elements in the true faith which could be known *only* by Tradition, without help from Scripture. This view is still strongly held by conservative Catholic theologians. The other view, that Scripture in a sense contains everything, but needs Tradition for its understanding and elucidation, began to appear again in the nineteenth century, and was in fact put forward by J. H. Newman in his celebrated reply to Dr Pusey.

If the conservatives are right, there is a deep doctrinal gulf between Catholicism and Protestantism on this fundamental point of our means of determining the true and full nature of the Christian revelation. If Newman is right, then we have a foundation for dialogue with Protestants. And this the more, since in non-Catholic ecumenical circles there is a growing tendency to revalue the role of Tradition—not as a supplement to Scripture, but as its interpreter.

The draft now under consideration, as I said above, leaves this question open, and will be criticized by conservatives for doing so. But it does something else of great theological importance. As against a theological position, which tended to reduce the Christian revelation to a system of true propositions, which it is the task of theology to understand and to develop by logical deduction, the new draft firmly adopts the position that God has revealed Himself by *deeds and words*, and supremely in and as the person of the historical Jesus. The development of the implications of this revelation is a matter not simply for theological deduction, but for a vital loving and unceasing *meditation*, for the trial-and-error process by which we grow in the knowledge of our friends by daily trustful intercourse with them; all this under the enlightening guidance of the Holy Ghost. One might quote Pascal: the heart has its reasons of which the understanding knows nothing. It may not be easy to provide a scientific proof from

Scripture of the truth of the Assumption of Our Lady; but the Church's heart, fed by that religious meditation of which she gave us an example when she "kept all these things and pondered them in her heart", has no doubt about this truth.

The Church addresses mankind as a body which has been authorized to relay a divine message: the Gospel or Good News from God. This message is the perpetual reannouncement of what God "spoke" in Palestine 1900 years ago: a message, a word, which *was* a historical person, one in nature with God for whom He spoke and with man to whom He spoke. Christ was the fullness of this message or revelation, and Christ is the burden of what the Church has to say to mankind today. He is a message which, it seems to us, the world urgently needs to hear and to ponder.

## 5. PRIESTLY LIFE AND SERVICE

*Conference given by the Right Reverend Gordon Wheeler, Coadjutor Bishop of Middlesbrough, 15th October 1964*

THIS CONFERENCE has attached to it little of the *éclat* of the great issues of the Second Vatican Council. The genealogy of the schema *"De Vita et Ministerio Sacerdotali"* descending from the earlier Ten Propositions (*De Sacerdotibus*) which, in turn emerged from three primary documents on the holiness of the Priestly Life, the duties and remuneration of the clergy, and their wider distribution according to the Church's needs, will indeed provide a synoptic exercise for future generations of somewhat obscure scholarship. And the different *relationes* will provide them with a fairly safe guide.

On the other hand, it would be dangerous to dismiss

the new schema as unimportant for several reasons. And without examining it in that detail which, any-how, is already available to you, I would like to indicate some of the notes which seem to me to have relevance for the *aggiornamento* in which, please God, we are all engaged.

In the first place, there is a new introduction which refers us back at once to *De Ecclesia* and *De Pastorali Episcoporum Munere* for the theological foundations. In section 28 of Chapter III of *De Ecclesia* and in section 3 of Chapter III of *De Pastorali Episcoporum Munere in Ecclesia*, the whole theology of the Priesthood in relation to the Episcopate, both in theory and practice, is clearly and succinctly delineated.

In the New Covenant there is really but one priest-hood; that of Christ. He is the One priest of the New Law as is made so clear to us in the Epistle to the Hebrews. And to study the Christian priesthood is to study the one priesthood of Christ in its fullest range. The Church equals the priestly Body of Christ, i.e. it is a sacerdotal organism because it is the extension of Christ the Priest.

As we know, there are two ways of sharing in Christ's priesthood: by Baptism and by Holy Order. Pope Pius XII in *Mediator Dei*, quoting Pope Innocent III, wrote: "Not only do priests offer, but all the Faithful offer too; what is performed in a special way by the ministry of the priests, is done in a general way by the desire of the Faithful".

"By the Sacrament of Holy Order the priest is ena-bled to perform an act of power and authority by which Christ is rendered present and the visible act of Sacri-fice accomplished. Considered in this way it is carried out by the priest alone: the laity do not share in the power of carrying out this act; nor does the priest possess this power as a mere deputy or representative of the people. The power comes to him by the character of Holy Order and in its exercise he is acting in the name of Christ and as His instrument, but that same visible act renders present the offering of Christ in which all are intended to share and which all must make their own.

"When Our Blessed Lord said: 'Do this in memory of me', with the added statement that He sent the Apostles as the Father had sent Him, He gave to the twelve the power themselves to celebrate the Eucharist as His own Eucharist and the power to provide for that celebration until the end of the world." By our ordination, then, we bishops and priests are raised to a unique relationship, and at-one-ment with the great High Priesthood of Christ Himself. So total is this union that we say in the Consecration of the Mass, "This is *my* Body; This is *my* Blood". And like Him and with Him, we are priests for ever.

Secondly (and this follows from the first point), the new schema, mindful of the new conception of "The People of God", and the closely knit sacerdotal relationship, stresses the importance of a *new dialogue*, if you like, between priests and people. Priest and laymen should work together in the mission of the Church, each regarding the other as a brother and fellow labourer in Christ, sharing in different measure in His priesthood.

Thank God—and I say this without being at all complacent—there has so far been a wonderful relationship between our priests and people which redounds to the credit of both. But let us not be blind to the fact that this cannot continue if the advice now given to us is disregarded.

The new conception of the "People of God", together with the high intellectual development of our laity, demands a priesthood of a kind which speaks and understands their language. This, to my mind, can only be achieved in the long run by a radical adaptation of seminary training to the ordinary national cultural institutions. If the dangerous dichotomy at present in existence continues, we shall only have ourselves to blame for the growth of an anti-clericalism from which we have been blessedly free.

I think our separated brethren have something to teach us in this matter.

Thirdly, all this in no way conflicts with the paramount place of a high spiritual, scriptural, patristic and pastoral formation.

The laity would never want their priests to be other than men apart. They want them above all to be men of prayer and wedded to the spirit of the Gospel. The new schema suitably commends an ever-increasing regard for the celibacy of the priestly life.

It is significant, is it not, that the Council, whilst passing a married diaconate by a considerable majority, held tenaciously to celibacy for the unmarried deacon and, by implication, for the priesthood. This, to my mind, is the right order of things. As one who has a great deal to do with convert clergy from other denominations or Churches, I welcome more than most legislation which may ultimately enable the married clergy to receive the diaconate and fulfil themselves in a truly pastoral function. Equally strongly, I am convinced—and this seems to be the mind of the Church as seen in the Council—that celibacy is one of the fairest jewels of the priesthood because, in itself, it is a high spiritual vocation and because it leaves a man unencumbered to exercise that pastoral freedom which "makes him a member of every family and yet belonging to none".

Fourthly, I welcome this schema because of its insistence on the traditional means of priestly sanctification enlightened by the new insights of the Liturgy. The writings of the Ancient Fathers on the priesthood are valid for all time precisely because of their scriptural and liturgical premises. On the other hand, almost every book written on the subject in the last 200 years needs rewriting. I do not allude to the great spiritual classics because they stand alone and are enhanced when the light of the Kerygma is brought to play upon them. But the rest shrivel up.

Finally, I quote from the *Ingoldsby Legends*:

"Never I ween
Was a prouder scene,
Read of in books or dreamt of in dreams
Than the Cardinal Lord Archbishop of Rheims".

How singularly fitting that the present Archbishop of Rheims should be the Relator to a schema which condemns outmoded feudalism and the whole world of the Little Jackdaw!

# 6. SCHEMA XIII

*Conference given by the Right Reverend George Dwyer, Bishop of Leeds, 22nd October 1964*

IT IS a commonplace by now to say that this is the schema everyone has been waiting for. It is expected that this at last is going to be practical. Liturgy, collegiality and the like are academic. Peace and war; social justice; marriage and family problems—these are the kind of questions which every man faces daily. What has the Church to say about them?

It would be a mistake, however, to think that this is the only schema which will have an immediate practical effect. The Liturgy Schema, for example, is not just about dressing up and acting in church. It has launched a movement which will uproot all kinds of age-old habits, cut psychological and emotional ties, shake to the foundations the ways of thought of three to four million Catholics—all this so that the emphasis on the individual's personal concern will give place to an emphasis on communal responsibility.

The schema on Ecumenism shifts the whole emphasis in our relations with other Christians on to the fact of our common baptism. Separated brethren still, but more brethren than separated.

Schema XIII also shifts an emphasis. All previous Councils spoke to Christendom only and spoke on the assumption that the audience was made up of either loyal sons or rebellious ones. In Schema XIII, for the first time, a Council addresses an audience which it does not assume to be necessarily Catholic or even Christian.

Schema XIII opens ambitiously. It paints a thumbnail sketch of the modern scene—knowledge growing faster than wisdom, materialism, frustration, even despair. Then it puts the crucial sentence: "No wonder that very many, whilst rightly proud of man's increasing control of nature, yet are beginning to doubt if history has any point or purpose."

In fact today, in the Western World at least, only Christians and Marxists conceive of history as working towards a goal. Very different goals, of course, for Christians and Marxists. But still both see a purpose in events. For the rest, history is simply one thing after another.

Now Schema XIII boldly asserts that the flux of history is the work of the Holy Spirit and that only with the light of the Holy Spirit can men discern the right way to guide events in co-operation with the Holy Spirit.

The way the schema tries to do this is by taking a number of practical problems, poverty, family, social justice, peace and war, and giving the Christian attitude to each.

The difficulties the schema has to face in working out this programme are formidable. They are by no means overcome as yet. The authors hope that the Council discussions will help. Therefore I would ask the Press to regard the schema very much as provisional. It is as yet only a basis for discussion.

One big difficulty is the audience. The schema says it is addressed to Catholics, other Christians, other believers in God, and indeed all men. But these very different men will be moved only by very different motives and arguments. There has already been criticism that the schema lays no deep doctrinal foundation. One may say: "How could it, if it is addressed to such a varied audience?" Doubtless the best way would be simply to state the Catholic attitude and Catholic reasons. Pope John told me in a private audience that he hoped the Council would work that way, that it would say to the world: "This is what we teach, this is how we view modern problems, what do you think about it?"

Some of the merits of the schema as it stands are:

1. It makes a real effort to show how the Church faces the paradox of being in the world, but not of it.

2. It affirms clearly that the world is good though flawed by sin and that the Church's place is in the midst of all human activity.

3. It tries to show how the Church must keep within its own sphere, e.g. co-operating with the State, but asking no privileges.

4. It faces a whole range of moral problems and

L

frankly admits that the full and immediate solution of all of them is not to hand.

5. It urges an open and generous policy of co-operation with all men of goodwill and discourages a policy of invariably launching parallel organizations when co-operation in existing organizations is possible.

Some of its defects are:

1. It is repetitive and wordy.

2. It does not clearly distinguish the various meanings of the word "world".

3. It does not treat of the other "finalistic" doctrine, namely, Dialectical Materialism.

It will be interesting to see whether a very large assembly, such as the Council, will be able to make a really cogent and trenchant document covering such a wide variety of subjects.

# 7. THE THIRD SESSION OF VATICAN II

*Conference given by Right Reverend Monsignor Lawrence McReavy, 19th November 1964*

THE DISTINCTIVE feature of this third session of the Council has been the sheer volume and diversity of the subject-matter discussed and voted upon by the Fathers. It is safe to say that never in the history of the Church have so many bishops debated and decided so many matters of grave moment in so short a time.

In 48 General Congregations (including tomorrow's), they have discussed, in whole or in part, no less than 13 schemata, namely, the two new chapters added to the Constitution on the Church (the eschatological aspect, and the Blessed Virgin Mary); the new preface and section on care of souls added to the decree on the Pastoral Function of Bishops; Religious Liberty; the Jews; Divine Revelation; the Lay Apostolate; the Priestly Life and Ministry; the Oriental Churches; the Church in the Modern World; Missionary Activity; Renewal and Adaptation of the Religious Life; the Training of Priests; Christian Education; and the Sacrament of Matrimony.

At the same time, while following or taking part in these debates, the Fathers have been called upon to express their will by vote on many of these documents, chapter by chapter, and in some cases section by section. In particular, the great Constitution on the Church, cardinal document of the whole Council, required no less than fifty-six ballots to get it through the first stage, and then, since the Fathers were free to add modifications to their final vote on each chapter as a whole and these were considered and in some cases incorporated by the Doctrinal Commission in the definitive version, a further eight votes were needed to approve the decisions of the Commission, plus a final vote, today, on the Constitution as a whole.

Moreover, in many cases, the Fathers had to hear and study explanatory reports from the Commissions designed to help them in making their decisions. For example, four lengthy reports preceded the voting on the controversial Chapter III which deals with the Hierarchical Constitution of the Church.

The explanation of all this intensive industry is not, of course, to be found in the spontaneous energy of the Fathers. Eager though most of them are to complete the work of the Council, they would almost certainly have liked more time to study the documents and reports piled upon them in an almost daily stream. The pressure came from the Co-ordinating Commission, aided and abetted by the Moderators.

Cardinal Tisserant, in his opening address to the first Congregation of this session, 15th September, expressed the desire of the Co-ordinating Commission to conclude the Council in this session and its belief that it could be done. It was for this end that all schemata not hitherto presented to the assembly had been drastically reduced to propositions during the interval following the second session, all except the schema on the Lay Apostolate. Further, in order to expedite the debates, any Father who desired to speak had to give five days' notice, plus a summary, and the Moderators were empowered to require Fathers whose points were similar to choose a common spokesman. And at the 9th Congregation (25th September) the Moderators issued a time-table of the submission of summaries which, when interpreted in the light of the rule of five days' previous notice, implied that the plan was, if possible, to complete the debates by about 23rd October, leaving the rest of the session for revision and voting.

For a while the debates were kept to schedule. The plan, if there was one, began to creak during the debate on the Lay Apostolate which was allowed to run on, somewhat repetitiously, for five Congregations (6th to 12th October), partly, it was surmised, because the only remaining schema due for full debate (The Church in the Modern World) was not yet ready for presentation. To allow even more time, two of the schemata of Propositions, the Priestly Life and Ministry and the Oriental Churches, were introduced ahead of schedule and discussed. When, however, the first of these, after a two-day debate, was sent back by the Fathers for revision and amplification into a full-length schema, it became evident that the original plan of finishing the Council in this session could not possibly be achieved. To judge from subsequent events, a new plan was then devised with the limited object of ensuring that all the remaining schemata would at least be presented and discussed sufficiently to enable the relevant Commissions to revise their texts in a manner likely to win the approval of the Fathers at a fourth session. This has allowed these schemata to receive a fuller degree of discussion than would have been possible under the original plan. So, for example, 12 Congregations were devoted to the debate on The Church in the Modern World, and an average of $2\frac{1}{2}$ to the rest. The schema of Propositions on The Missionary Activity of the Church, like that on the Priestly Life and Ministry, was sent back, by 1601 votes to 311, for revision and amplification.

Even if these revised documents are eventually submitted to fresh discussion, a short fourth session, a few weeks, should now suffice to complete the work of the Council. Had the same degree of pressure that has characterized this third session been applied from the first, three sessions would have been ample. But there would have been reasonable ground for complaint and regret.

# V. CLOSURE OF THE
THIRD SESSION

*Address of His Holiness Pope Paul VI*

VENERABLE BRETHREN,

These last two months have been filled with hard work, the work of brothers, and now we must thank God for the happiness of celebrating this Second Vatican Ecumenical Council: now that we are rounding off the labours of its Third Session with all the solemnity of this sacred meeting. It is no exaggeration to say that it is our bounden duty to express to God our heartfelt, joyful awareness of His kindness: for He has given us the unique privilege of taking part in this historic, forward-looking event. We must thank Him too for giving me the privilege, in the leading role which in all humility I have the good fortune to sustain, of giving it its importance, its meaning and its completion. Impossible not to apply to ourselves the Lord's words, "Blessed are your eyes for they have sight: blessed are your ears for they have hearing" (Matt. 13. 16).

### The Sacred Hierarchy United in a Single Prayer, Faith and Charity

I see before me, in the mind's eye, God's Holy Church mustered with the help of my voice, gathered in its flocks around the Pastors who represent it. Here is the Catholic Hierarchy, whose job it is to give formation and guidance to the holy People of God; it gathers here visibly in one place with a single aspiration, a single prayer, a single faith, a single charity on the lip and in the heart. The gathering before me is beyond compare; I do not cease to marvel at it; I shall never be able to forget it. For the glory of the Father, Son and Spirit is the goal of its striving; its aim has been the recalling of Revelation's high message, the deep scrutiny of its deepest significance. The men gathered here in a single body are strangers, as no one else has ever been, to self-interest and triviality. No one else has ever been as intent as they on bearing witness to divine truth. Of course they are weak and subject to error, they are men; but they are convinced that they can proclaim truths which cannot be disputed, truths which have no end. They are men of this age, children of this earth, but transcending earth and time to shoulder their brothers' burdens, to bring them to spiritual safety. Men endowed with the will to devote themselves completely; men fired with a love which is more extensive than the hearts in which it burns; men under an impulse, which may possibly seem rash, but it is combined with a calm confidence that they are inquiring into the meaning of human life and history, that they are giving it its importance, extension, beauty, unity in Christ—in Christ the Lord alone. Here is something to marvel at, Venerable Brethren here present. This is something to marvel at, you men whose eyes are fixed on us from outside. Ask yourselves the question: Will we ever have the chance of seeing a greater spectacle, a more religious, more heart-stirring sight?

Now we have reached the final moment of the Council session; we are about to bring it to a close. The joy that we feel is increased if we recall in memory the theme of our discussions, the subject-matter of our Constitution. The doctrine on the Church has been studied and expounded; this has been to complete the doctrinal work of the First Vatican Ecumenical Council. The mystery of the Church and the divine plan in its fundamental constitution have been probed.

## Catholic Doctrine on the Episcopate

We must, I repeat, thank God for this happy outcome. It is right that a feeling of joy should pervade our hearts. It is going to be easier from now on to understand the Mind of God as it bears on the Mystical Body of Christ. From this understanding we are going to be able to derive clearer, surer rules for the life of the Church, as well as an increase of strength to help her ceaseless efforts to bring men to salvation, and a greater hope for the progress of Christ's Kingdom in the world. And we should praise God for it.

The work performed; the pious zeal, the eagerness to see that it was in full accord with the truth contained in Sacred Scripture and in the Church's genuine tradition; the hard work to discover the fundamental truth of the Church's constitutional law, to distinguish between what is fixed and unalterable and what derives from its origins by way of a lawful, natural development; the desire to throw light on the Church's mystery from every angle, to bring light equally to all the parts of the Mystical Body, to all its functions, to all the purposes for which it strives—it would take a long speech to deal with all these topics.

All the same, the hardest section of this spiritual toil, the treatment of the doctrine of the Episcopate, is also the most memorable. I may therefore be justified in expressing briefly my feelings on this chapter alone.

I want to make it clear that it was a great pleasure to me that in the handling of this doctrine abundant opportunity was given for study and discussion, and that there was a corresponding clarity in its conclusions. The completion of the First Vatican Ecumenical Council was certainly necessary; the right moment had arrived. It was demanded by the great increase of theological studies in our time and by the spread of the Catholic Church all over the world. Questions arising out of the daily exercise of pastoral zeal required an answer from the Church. Bishops wanted an explanation of the doctrine which concerns their own position. The method adopted was well suited to the task: so much so that I have no hesitation, taking into consideration the explanation (in the Appendices) of the interpretation of the words used, and of the theological force that the Council intended the proposed doctrine to be given—I have, I say, no hesitation in publishing, with the help of God, this Constitution on the Church.

The best comment on this promulgation seems to be that it has brought about no change in traditional teaching. Christ's intention is our intention; what was in existence still exists. The teaching of the Church in the years that have rolled by is our teaching too. The only difference is that what was previously only lived in practice is now clearly expressed as teaching; what previously was the subject of examination, discussion and, to some extent, of dispute has now been reduced to the certainty of formulated doctrine. It would be true for us to say that God's Providence has given us the radiance of this shining hour: I mean the hour which yesterday was slow in coming; today it shows a blaze of light; tomorrow its saving power will enrich the Church with the freshness of its addition to doctrine, an increase of strength, a better adaptation of teaching.

### The Vocation, Sanctification and Government of the People of God

It is a pleasure too to observe the honour that this document pays to the People of God. Nothing could delight me more than the sight of the solemn acknowledgement of the dignity of all my Brethren, of all my Children who make up the *plebs sancta*. The whole of the ministry of the Hierarchy is orientated towards the vocation, the sanctification, the government, the eternal salvation of the People of God as its objective. I am equally comforted by the decrees of this Constitution on my Brethren in the Episcopate. I cannot describe my joy to see the solemnity with which their dignity is proclaimed, their functions celebrated and recognition given to their power. I cannot say how grateful I am to God for my good fortune, for it is I who am to render the honour due to the sacredness of your ministry, the fullness of your priesthood, and to proclaim the solidarity which binds you to me, Venerable and beloved Brethren.

Something else that I have noticed has given me pleasure and edification. This document contains, at more than one point, full recognition and respect for the original, universal, individual office given by Christ the Lord to Peter and transmitted to the Roman Pontiffs, his successors—the office I hold at the present time despite my unworthiness. Impossible that I should not be pleased: not for the honour which it reflects on me, for I find this great office formidable; I am not attached to it by desire. It is the honour shown to the words of Christ that pleases me, and the renewed assertion of harmony with Sacred Tradition and the Church's *Magisterium*. A final reason for my pleasure is the guarantee it gives of protection to the unity of the Church, to the uniformity and efficiency of her action which is entirely dependent for its security on the Church's government. It was of the greatest importance that these prerogatives of the Supreme Pontificate be recognized with clarity and precision, when it came to the solution of the problem of episcopal authority in the Church. The problem had to be solved in such a way that episcopal authority could be seen in no sense to oppose, but rather to be in full accord with the power of the Vicar of Christ, the Head of the Episcopal College, as the constitutional law of the Church demands.

### The Perfect Union of All the Pastors with Peter's Successor

This close, essential connection makes a single unified body of the Episcopate. The Bishop who is Peter's successor does not oppose it with an alien power; on the contrary he is its head and centre. That is why I am anxious to proclaim your rights together with my own, to rejoice at their increase, to assert their excellence, and to crown them and mine alike with completion.

When, in this way, I acknowledge the plenary, effective power of the episcopal office, my attention is drawn to the growing fellowship of faith, charity, responsibility and help that surrounds me. Thus in recognizing and exalting your authority, I am not afraid that my own is going to decrease or be obstructed. On the contrary, I feel an access of strength from the affection that makes us brothers. I feel an extra fitness in addressing myself to the task of governing the universal Church, since I am aware that each of you shares my aspirations. I feel my confidence in the help of Jesus Christ growing because of our close association in His name, and because of my hope that this association will continue in the future.

### The Increased Radiance of the "Mother and Teacher"

It is not easy to visualize at the moment the practical results which are likely to follow from the declaration of this doctrine. It is not hard to foresee, however, that it will bear a crop of spiritual studies and canonical regulations. The Ecumenical Council will be concluded with the next session, its fourth. To carry its decrees into practice, a number of Post-Conciliar Commissions will have to be erected and the Episcopate will have to help in directing them. I have the same scheme in mind for dealing with business of general interest—the characteristic of our age—which is continually cropping up. I shall be increasingly prepared to send for a number of you, who are yet to be chosen, Venerable Brethren, at fixed times, and to take them into consultation. I do not want to go without the comfort of your presence, the help of your prudence and experience, the support of your advice or your authoritative approval. A useful result of this procedure will be that the Roman Curia, which is to be reshaped—a matter receiving careful attention—will be able to draw on the experience of Diocesan Pastors. Its loyal service already secures efficiency, but in this way it will be able to perfect the acquittal of its duties with the help of Bishops from different areas who will come and assist with their wisdom and charity.

The increase in the number of studies and discussions may present a practical difficulty, since collective action is more complicated than that of individuals. But if it corresponds more closely with the character of the Church—at one and the same time a monarchy and a hierarchy—and if it means a lightening of my labours by means of your helpful service, we will find the prudence and the charity to overcome the characteristic difficulties of this more involved form of government.

I look forward to many good results in the souls of men, especially of Catholics, from the doctrine of the mystery of the Church, now that the Second Vatican Council has made its illuminating statement. The real face of the Bride of Christ shows up more clearly now and all Christ's faithful should be able to see it. They should be able to see the beauty of their Mother and Teacher, to see the majestic simplicity of this venerable foundation. They should be able to admire the near-miracle of her historic faith, her glorious social life, her excellent legislation; to admire also the significant progress of the Kingdom. Here it is that the divine and human elements are interwoven to produce in the society of the men who believe in Christ the bright reflection of the Divine Plan of the Incarnation and the Resurrection: so that the whole Christ our Saviour, may be seen, to borrow St Augustine's phrase.

### Cordial Wishes and Greetings to Other Brothers in Christ

Those who make of Christian perfection their single, consistent profession, should be especially delighted at this agreeable spectacle. I am referring to Religious, men and women, the best organs of the Church, her noble defenders, her dearest children.

Some of my Brethren and Children live in countries where they are at the present time denied any adequate, worthwhile religious liberty, or where it is so restricted that we have to enrol them in the Church of Silence or the Church of Tears. They must also find reason for joy in this spectacle. They should be delighted with the splendour of the doctrine which throws light on the Church to which they are giving the splendid witness of their endurance of hardship, the witness of their active loyalty. The glory they are winning in so doing is of the highest degree; it is like the glory of Christ, Victim for the redemption of mankind.

I am prompted to the further hope that our separated Brethren in Christ will give this doctrine their balanced and kind consideration. I cannot say how much I hope that this doctrine, in conjunction with the complementary explanations contained in the Schema "*De Oecumenismo*" which the Council has approved in like manner, will be a leaven of love; I hope that it will rouse their hearts to a reappraisal of their plans and intentions, that they may draw nearer and nearer to our fellowship and finally, when God grants it, merge with us in it. Meanwhile the doctrine makes a pleasing impression on my mind: for I notice that the Church, in tracing her own features, is in no sense narrowing the scope of her charity, but rather enlarging it; nor does she check the manifold impulse of her catholicity which is always advancing, constantly beckoning. Here I beg permission to greet the Observers representing separated Churches and Christian Persuasions, to tender my gratitude for their willingness to attend the Council meetings and to wish them prosperity.

My final wish would be that the sacred doctrine of the Church might reflect some of its joyful light on the surrounding, secular world in which she lives. It ought to present itself as the sign lifted up to the nations (cf. Is. 5. 26) for the safe guidance of all men on their journey to the truth and to the attainment of life. Obviously the austere scientific procedure of Theology has the first claim on the elaboration of this doctrine, for Theology is responsible for its justification and proclamation. Nevertheless it is not unconcerned with the human race. The human race is mingled with the Church, it provides the historical and social context in which she discharges her function; it is the *raison d'être* of the Church's foundation. The Church claims no other authority on earth than that which allows her to serve men and love them.

The Holy Church may be perfecting her own thought, her own structure, but she is not making herself remote from the experience of the men of her day. She is rather concerned to reach an understanding of them, to share their hardships and their legitimate hopes, and to support their efforts to attain prosperity, peace and freedom.

I intend to return to this theme at the end of the Council when in the next session, which is to be the last, there will be a full treatment of the Schema "On Religious Liberty" and the other Schema "On the Church in the Modern World". Shortage of time alone made it impossible to deal with the former before the end of this session, and the latter, which has already been glanced at in this session and is to complete the work of the Council.

### A Matchless Hymn of Praise in Honour of Mary

Before I conclude, I have another attractive subject in mind.

We cannot possibly proceed with the agenda, Venerable Brethren, without some thought for the Most Blessed Virgin Mary, without the wholehearted gratitude that children should have. We like, after all, to reckon her the protector of the Council, the witness of our labours, the counsellor who commands our love. We did, after all, commit our labours at the outset of the Council to her heavenly patronage and that of St Joseph (cf. *A.A.S.*, LIII, 1961, pp. 37 f., 211 ff.; LIV, 1962, p. 727).

This was the thought in our minds when we gathered in the Liberian Basilica last year, in front of the painting with the glorious title, "Salvation of the Roman People", and paid honour to the Bountiful Mother of God.

More splendid still, and more significant, is the honour that the Council wants to pay her this year. The very headstone of the Constitution *De Ecclesia*, to be published today, is the chapter dealing with the Blessed Virgin Mary. We are entitled to say that this session is being concluded with a matchless hymn in praise of the Virgin Mother of God.

For the very first time—and it is not without emotion that I make this statement—an Ecumenical Council has produced a synthesis, a rich synthesis, of the Catholic teaching on the place to be assigned to the Blessed Virgin Mary in the Mystery of Christ and the Church.

This marks no departure from the avowed intention of the Council to show the face of Holy Church. The Mother of God is closely connected with the Church: she is, to borrow a remarkable phrase, its "greatest part, finest part, principal part, choicest part" (Rupert, *in Apoc.* I, VII, c. 12: *P.L.*, 169, 1043-4).

Hierarchical structure, Sacred Liturgy, Sacraments, framework of Laws—these things alone do not make the Church. She has an essential inner power, the source of the sanctification she brings effectively to men; and this power is based on her mystical union with Christ. Impossible, then, to think of this union without thinking of the woman who is Mother of the Word made flesh, the woman of whom Christ made an intimate associate to win us salvation.

The Church is in our sights while we gaze, as we ought, with love on the wonders wrought by God in His Holy Mother. Understanding of the true Catholic teaching on the Blessed Virgin Mary will always be an effective approach to the right understanding of the Mystery of Christ and the Church.

Mary's close connection with the Church has been clearly explained in the Council's Constitution. It convinces me that, with all its solemnity, this is the opportune moment to fulfil a wish. A great number of the Fathers have taken up the hint I gave of my wish at the end of the last session. They have made an urgent request that there should be, in the course of the Council, an explicit proclamation of the motherly function which the Blessed Virgin Mary sustains among the Christian people. This has made me decide to introduce at this public meeting the title which is to honour the Blessed Virgin Mary. The title has been the subject of request from different parts of the world. I myself am particularly pleased with it, for it is a remarkably concise expression of the outstanding position of the Mother of God in the Church, the position which the Council has recognized to belong to her personally.

## *Mother of the Church, Pray for Us*

In honour, therefore, of the Blessed Virgin and for our comfort, I proclaim Mary Most Holy to be the Mother of the Church, Mother, in other words, of the whole Christian people, faithful and Pastors alike, who call her their loving mother. I decree, also, that the whole Christian people should make use of this attractive title to increase the honour of the Mother of God in the prayers that they offer.

The title in question is no novelty to Christian piety: Christ's faithful and the whole Church have shown a preference for calling upon Mary by the name of Mother. The name has a real place in genuine Marian devotion, for this devotion is based on Mary's dignity as Mother of the Word of God made flesh.

The Divine Motherhood is the reason for her unique relationship with Christ, and for her presence at the performance by Christ Jesus of the work of man's salvation. So too, the Divine Motherhood is the origin of the relationship between Mary and the Church. Mary is the Mother of Christ: the moment He took a human nature in her virginal womb, He joined Himself as Head to His Mystical Body, the Church. As Mother of Christ, Mary must be reckoned the Mother, too, of all the faithful and Pastors, that is to say Mother of the Church.

## Lively Confidence for the Whole Human Race

This is the reason we have for lifting our eyes to her with the warm, confident love of children, despite our weakness, despite our unworthiness. She once gave us Jesus, the source of heavenly grace; she cannot fail to help the Church, now especially, to make livelier efforts as Christ's Bride to fulfil her saving function.

This confidence is further developed and corroborated by reflection on the close bonds between our heavenly Mother and the whole human race. God has endowed her with a wealth of remarkable gifts to make of her the worthy Mother of God: she is still very close to us. She is, like us, a child of Adam; this makes her our sister, since she shares our human nature. In view of the merits of Christ, she was exempted from original sin; to the gifts that she received from God she added her personal faith which was total and exemplary: it prompted the cry of praise in the Gospel, "Blessed art thou for thy believing".

In this mortal life she portrayed the perfect model of a disciple of Christ, the mirror of all virtues, the embodiment of the beatitudes which Christ Jesus preached. And so, the Church, for the development of her many sided life and activity, takes the Virgin Mother of God as the perfect example of the Imitation of Christ.

When the Constitution *De Ecclesia* is duly published, and I have given it its finishing touch by proclaiming Mary "Mother of all the Faithful and Pastors" or "Mother of the Church", I am quite sure that the whole Christian people will call upon the Blessed Virgin with increased hope and fervour and render her the cult and honour that she deserves.

As for us, our first entry into this Council Chamber, in obedience to my predecessor John XXIII, was made together with "Mary, the Mother of Jesus". We ought, in the same way, to take our departure from this church in the most holy and delightful name of Mary, Mother of the Church.

To show your gratitude for the motherly aid which Mary has given us throughout this session, each one of you should strive to raise her name and honour higher in the eyes of the Christian people. You should put her example before them for their imitation—her example of faith, of ready response to any movement of heavenly grace, of a life modelled on Christ's teaching and the inspiration of charity. It should be your aim that all the faithful, united in the name of the Mother that they have in common, should have a greater sensation of steadiness in the profession of their faith and the following of Christ. They should be more charitable towards their brethren by improving their love of the poor, their zeal for justice, their defence of peace. The standard has already been set by the great St Ambrose, "Each individual should have Mary's soul to praise the Lord, Mary's spirit to rejoice in God" (St Ambrose, *Expos. in Luc. II, 26;* P.L., 15, 1642).

### A Golden Rose for the Shrine of Our Lady of Fatima

There is one point that I am anxious to see set in a clear light: everything about Mary, the lowly handmaid of the Lord, has its full significance in Jesus Christ, the sole Mediator, our Redeemer. I am equally desirous that a clear explanation be given of the real nature and intent of the cult due to the Virgin Mary, especially in districts which contain a large number of our separated brethren. I want all those outside the Catholic Church to understand that devotion to the Virgin Mother of God is not to be reckoned an end in itself, but a means of guiding men to Christ and of uniting them with the Eternal Father in the Holy Spirit's bond of charity.

We are lifting our hearts in fervent prayer to the Blessed Virgin Mary to ask her good prayers for the Ecumenical Council and the Holy Church, to hasten the long awaited moment when all the followers of Christ may at last be reunited. Meanwhile we turn our eyes to the vast extent of the whole world: the whole world which is the beloved object of this Ecumenical Synod's keen attention: the whole world which my predecessor Pius XII was inspired to dedicate solemnly to the Immaculate Heart of the Virgin Mary. I have considered it right to commemorate this consecration in a special way. With this in mind I have decided to send a special mission to take a Golden Rose to the Shrine at Fatima which is so dear to the people of Portugal—who have always had my special love and today more than ever—but known too and respected among the faithful of the whole Catholic community. In this way I am putting the whole human race under the protective care of our heavenly Mother, with all its difficulties, anxieties, just aspirations and fervent hopes.

### *Invocation to the Immaculate Queen of the Universe*

Virgin Mother of God, august Mother of the Church, may I entrust the whole Church and the Ecumenical Council to you.

You have the happy name of "Help of the Bishops"; keep them safe in the watch they keep over their office. Their pastoral office gives them a difficult role to sustain, stand by them and the priests, religious and layfolk who support them with their efforts.

Remember all your children. Add to their prayers the unique power of your influence with God. Keep their faith constant and intact, strengthen their hope, give fire to their charity.

Remember those who are in difficulty, need and danger, especially those who are harassed and imprisoned for the Christian faith. Obtain courage for their hearts and hasten, Virgin Mother, the day of deliverance that they wait for.

Turn your eyes with kindness on our separated Brethren. You gave birth to Christ, the bridge of Unity between God and man, please join us and them again one day.

You are a shrine of pure light, untouched by shadow; through your Son we have attained reconciliation with the Father (cf. Rom. 5. 11), ask Him to show mercy to our errors, to keep the whole world from division to give our hearts the joy of loving the brethren.

Virgin Mother of God, may I commend the whole human race to your Immaculate Heart. Bring it to a recognition of Christ Jesus, the sole, true Saviour. Keep it from the disastrous effects of sin, furnish it with the peace that consists in truth, justice, freedom and love.

Grant the whole Church, in celebrating this great Ecumenical Synod, the strength to sing a solemn hymn of praise and thanksgiving to the mercy of God, a hymn of exultant joy that He who is mighty has wrought wonders through your instrumentality, "O CLEMENS, O PIA, O DULCIS VIRGO MARIA".